PRENTICE-HALL SERIES
IN WORLD RELIGIONS

ROBERT S. ELLWOOD, JR., ED

BEYOND "THE PRIMITIVE"
THE RELIGIONS OF NONLITERATE PEOPLES
———————————————————————————— *SAM D. GILL*

HINDUISM: A CULTURAL PERSPECTIVE
———————————————————————————— *DAVID R. KINSLEY*

ISLAM: A CULTURAL PERSPECTIVE
———————————————————————————— *RICHARD C. MARTIN*

BEYOND
"THE PRIMITIVE"
the religions of
nonliterate peoples

Sam D. Gill

University of Colorado– Boulder

BEYOND "THE PRIMITIVE" the religions of nonliterate peoples

Prentice-Hall, Inc., Englewood Cliffs, New Jersey 07632

Library of Congress Cataloging in Publication Data

GILL, SAM D. (DATE)
   Beyond the primitive.

   (The Prentice-Hall series in world religions)
   Bibliography:
   Includes index.
   I. Religion, Primitive. I. Title.
   II. Series: Prentice-Hall series in world
religions.
GN470.G5   306'6   81–5913
ISBN 0–13–076034–X   AACR2

Interior/cover design by Maureen Olsen
Editorial production/supervision by Frank Hubert
Manufacturing buyer: Harry P. Baisley

© 1982 by Prentice-Hall, Inc., Englewood Cliffs, N.J. 07632

Printed in the United States of America

10 9 8 7 6 5

Prentice-Hall International, Inc., *London*
Prentice-Hall of Australia Pty. Limited, *Sydney*
Prentice-Hall of Canada, Ltd., *Toronto*
Prentice-Hall of India Private Limited, *New Delhi*
Prentice-Hall of Japan, Inc., *Tokyo*
Prentice-Hall of Southeast Asia Pte. Ltd., *Singapore*
Whitehall Books Limited, *Wellington, New Zealand*

for Corbin Matthew

Contents

Foreword

The Prentice-Hall Series in World Religions is a new set of introductions to the major religious traditions of the world, which intends to be distinctive in two ways: (1) Each book follows the same outline, allowing a high level of consistency in content and approach. (2) Each book is oriented toward viewing religious traditions as ''religious cultures'' in which history, ideologies, practices, and sociologies all contribute toward constructing ''deep structures'' that govern peoples' world view and life-style. In order to achieve this level of communication about religion, these books are not chiefly devoted to dry recitations of chronological history or systematic exposition of ideology, though they present overviews of these topics. Instead the books give considerable space to ''cameo'' insights into particular personalities, movements, and historical moments that encourage an understanding of the world view, life-style, and deep dynamics of religious cultures in practice as they affect real people.

Religion is an important element within nearly all cultures, and itself has all the hallmarks of a full cultural system. ''Religious culture'' as an integrated complex includes features ranging from ideas and organization to dress and diet. Each of these details offers some insight into the meaning of the whole as a total experience and construction of a total ''reality.'' To look at the religious life of a particular country or tradition in this way, then, is to give proportionate attention to all aspects of its manifestation: to thought, worship, and social organization; to philosophy and folk beliefs; to liturgy and pilgrimage; to family life, dress, diet, and the role of religious specialists like monks and shamans. This series hopes to instill in the minds of readers the ability to view religion in this way.

I hope you enjoy the journeys offered by these books to the great heartlands of the human spirit.

ROBERT S. ELLWOOD, JR., editor
University of Southern California

Preface

There has been an explosion of interest in the nonliterate peoples who live in small isolated communities the world over. It was set off in the nineteenth century as the idea of evolution in natural history began to transform the study of culture and humanity and as expanding travel and communication began to shrink the world, bringing all peoples closer together. Ethnography, which arose as a field devoted to the scientific recording of these cultures, added greatly to the information gathered by missionaries and travelers. The thousands of volumes produced during a period of little more than a century are an impressive achievement. The emphasis has often been on collecting data to save some trace, some record, of peoples who, with the rest of the world, were undergoing change at an unprecedented rate. Many of those peoples living in relatively small communities subsisting mainly upon what they could produce have not survived the rapid advance of modernity. Written records, perhaps hastily collected, are often the only remains of a culture. Yet many peoples have survived and have shown remarkable tenacity and adaptability in the face of these forces of change, but there are few if any cultures left in the world who are untouched by modernity.

Religion has such a prominent place in the records of these peoples that few observers have failed to appreciate its importance. This constant presence of religion in all human communities has encouraged many Western students of culture to ponder the role and character of religion in human history. The result has been a considerable transformation in the study of religion. Throughout most of the period in which these data have generated such interesting questions, hardened and established views or schools of thought have dictated that the religions of nonliterate peoples be seen in particular ways. These cultures have been considered as laboratories and the published records about them as fields of data to be freely used by the proponent of any theory in order to show proof for his or her view or to criticize the view of another. This has often produced unfortunate results, but despite these difficulties it has provided many of the terms and approaches currently used by students of religion, especially those engaged in comparative and cultural studies of religion. Even with the wealth of available resources and the potential importance of these studies, only a few religion scholars are presently engaged in studying the religions of nonliterate peoples. The subject has remained of interest to students, however, and it continues to be one of the most stimulating and effective ways of introducing the subject of religious studies.

In writing this book I have wanted to achieve many things, but central has been my concern to establish a suitable ground upon which members of Western literate cultures may stand to better comprehend and appreciate the religions of the many small communities of nonliterate peoples. We commonly identify these peoples by the term *primitive* and since I strongly believe that this term has greatly misshaped the average person's view of these peoples, I cannot begin this task without attempting some resolution to this terminological issue. All is lost if we do not first take into account the ideas, images, and expectations the reader may bring to this book. Only in this way can we hope to be free of the prejudices we may hold unaware. Other authors have concerned themselves with the use of this term, but commonly settle the matter by making a disclaimer to indicate that they do not mean that the peoples so called are really primitive in most senses of the word. They usually accept established usage, compensating for the errors it perpetuates by placing the term in quotation marks. I have not been able to accept this as a solution. To retain the term *primitive* would, for me, be a use of language which would violate one of the most precious lessons we have to learn in the study of these cultures, which is that the use of language is very influential in how we perceive the world, even in how the world is created.

This rejection has forced me to search for alternative terminology and that, in turn, has required that I try to justify it. I attempt this task in the introductory chapter. Seeking new terminology has encouraged me to emphasize certain aspects of these religious traditions which I feel are important to our efforts to understand them; most central among these is their emphasis on the importance of the oral and nonverbal dimensions of culture, that is, their nonliteracy. There are many other important aspects of these cultures which might serve as focus, but at the least I hope to achieve a presentation of these religious cultures in terms which do not deeply prejudice our interpretations, and certainly not on the basis of a highly value-laden view of religion and culture. But the advancement beyond "the primitive" is not simply a terminological goal, it is a general goal for the level of our understanding.

In advancing our appreciation of nonliterate peoples beyond our own predispositions about "the primitive," I hope to show that nonliterate cultures are closer to literate Western cultures than we have commonly recognized. In the long history of exploiting certain aspects of the former, differences between "us" and "them" have been so emphasized that it has become difficult for us to see the common areas shared by all humans. We can no longer learn from the experience of our encounter. We must move beyond "the primitive" in order that we not consider the religions of nonliterate peoples simply a curiosity. This is particularly important at a time when differences are being broadly exploited as the bizarre and the incredible.

Yet although common ground must exist, I stress that I am not in the least interested in discounting differences to show that after all we are all the same. It is through the richness and diversity of religions that we come to know the character of religion as a dimension of culture and humanity and consequently that we may hope to understand any single tradition, including our own, more deeply.

In writing this book I have attempted to avoid forms of presentation which hide, obscure, or dull the subjects. Often in our eagerness to do our best to explain and interpret our subjects, we forget to present them sufficiently and we lose the richness and feeling which can survive even in written descriptions. Yet the religions of nonliterate peoples cannot be adequately understood simply by reading descriptions no matter how accurate and lively they may be, nor can we often adequately understand unfamiliar religious events simply because we have observed them first hand. Still, as many examples as possible should be presented and I have endeavored to include a wide variety. I have attempted to guide the reader to some understanding of these specific examples, but in order that the reader might be directed to questions about the character of religion wherever it is found, I have centered theoretical and interpretive discussions upon these specific examples. I have endeavored to equip the reader to approach the people in nonliterate cultures, either in person or through the use of the enormous ethnographic record, with some ideas about how to meet and to understand their religious events and beliefs.

In many ways the writing of this book has been personal, and consequently it doubtless bears more of my prejudices than I fully recognize. Despite the dangers which must accompany this possibility, I know no alternative and I accept that responsibility. Although I hope that in some ways this book will contribute to the academic study of religion, I will be satisfied if it introduces students to this fascinating area of study and engages them in new questions about the nature of religion.

I want to thank Robert S. Ellwood, Jr., for inviting me to write this book. His support and direction have been most helpful. Through his careful reading of the manuscript, my colleague, Joel Gereboff, has contributed much to it. My wife, Judy, discussed with me many an idea related to the work and shared my enthusiasm for it. I thank her for this as well as for her careful readings of the manuscript. Many have influenced my views of religion and my approach to the study of religion, but none so much as Jonathan Z. Smith. Since his influence stands unacknowledged behind much of this book I wish here to acknowledge him and to express my admiration and respect for his work.

SAM D. GILL

*BEYOND
"THE PRIMITIVE"
the religions of
nonliterate peoples*

into the forest dimly:
an introduction

We must enter into a relationship with people when we study their religions and cultures. Granted this is something of a peculiar relationship when we must meet them only in our imaginations, stimulated and informed by what we glean from a printed page. When our subjects are the peoples we have commonly identified by the term *primitive,* we often falter with their names and must consult an atlas to try to figure out where they live, or *lived* as is often the case. We are at once repelled and attracted by the strangeness or the alien character of their ways. In such a relationship we must realize that because of the way in which we necessarily meet these "other peoples," we are the active party. Consequently, the way we come to this meeting—equipped by our own history, language, ideas, and culture—greatly determines the nature of our experience. The religions and cultures we will meet in this book are trapped in print, and the peoples have no opportunity to present themselves or to protest our misunderstandings of them. Thus, we have a special obligation to carefully examine the perspectives and expectations we bring to such a meeting, for only we can guard against the disservice which our own views can do to those whom we will meet.

"THE PRIMITIVE"

The peoples we will be considering in this book have commonly been identified by the term *primitive.* For any person in Western culture, this term evokes a series of images with which we have considerable experience, even if we have never encountered any of the actual peoples. Since these images of "the primitive" will affect how we view the subjects of this book, they must be examined.

One group of images evoked by the term *primitive* is that of the caveman. Here we imagine a dark, gaping cave with looming shadows cast by a flickering fire upon the vaulted walls. We see, hunched behind the fire, a group of figures, garments of hide slung from one shoulder. They are stooped, squat, thick-boned. Their eyes are dark, the brow protruding, the hair matted. Our image may include red meat being gnawed from large bones and babies on the floor playing with discarded bones or mongrel dogs. We may picture the women being dragged by the hair at the mercy of a cave Romeo shouldering a club. The lives of such people, we tend to think, would surely be directed by forces of magic and superstition.

Another group of images commonly evoked by the term *primitive* is that of the *native.* Our images of "natives" may well have been nurtured by the photographs of *National Geographic,* which has brought us a steady stream of these peoples. With each issue of the magazine we have been delighted by the "natives" who stand minimally clad, decorations of bones piercing noses or ears, against the background of their modest huts. There seem always to be pictures of things they choose for food and the ways they go about acquiring and preparing them. All is wonderfully strange to us. Pictured are colorfully costumed dances which must be inspired by magic or superstition. The apparent impoverishment these peoples endure seems to justify our use of the term *primitive* to describe them. They appear to be still in the primal or first station of human history.

Given the extent to which the images associated with the term *primitive* appear in our lives we must realize that this figure is deeply embedded in our literature and lore. It appears in many forms in Saturday morning television cartoons; it is recurrent in literature and film; and there is a whole genre of comic strips and cartoons about "natives" and "cave people" that appears in newspapers and magazines from *Playboy* to *The New Yorker.* The images we recognize by the term *the primitive* are a part of our own history and culture and, at least in terms of our images, may have little to do with any actual peoples.

When we examine the character of our primitive we find a complex ambivalence. On the one hand, he is everything we aren't, everything we despise. On the other hand, he is everything that we are, everything we admire. Whereas we are wise, sophisticated, and civilized, he is foolish, crude, naive, and savage. We are logical, literate, technological, and modern. He has yet to enter these stages of human development. Notably we often use the prefix *pre* to describe him, for we see him only in a precedent-antecedent relationship with ourselves. However, in contrast, he is like us in carrying the germ of culture; indeed, in much of our lore, he is the bringer of culture. We look to him to understand language, social structure, economic and political systems, the psyche, humor, and even intellection. We see him as the cosmographer and chronographer who first made conscious orientation in space and time. In our primitive we can find the nature of culture and humankind in its basic forms.

When we are disenchanted with our culture, its complexities and mistakes, we may see our primitive as wholly natural, as sons and daughters of the earth and sky, brothers and sisters of the plants and animals, living entirely by nature's ways, part of the ecological system, never upsetting its delicate balance.

Although our primitive is sometimes the dupe, the fool, the negative image of all that we are, he is us, still in the kernel, our ancestor, our culture hero, our prototype.

In short, what I am suggesting is that our images of "the primitive" are not accurate reports of actual peoples who live in small communities upon the products of their own efforts. Our primitive, although perhaps inspired by some of the appearances of these peoples, is nonetheless a figure created by the great loremakers of the late nineteenth and early twentieth centuries to meet the urgent needs which arose in that period of our history. That needful situation was bred in the Enlightenment. It involved the discovery of the almost infinite depth of time and breadth of space, the rise of natural history as the base for reality, the decline of the role of God, and the increasing awareness of peoples who appeared to be very unlike us. We found ourselves in an entirely new world. We found it difficult to know any longer who we were, and we needed help.

The creation of our primitive helped us in the way we most urgently needed; he helped us to know ourselves. He has done this in both positive and negative ways. He is subject to the tricks of our missionaries, colonists, and cowboys—a buffoon, a fool, crude physically, sexually, and intellectually. But he showed us that we have come to be what we are because long ago, before advancing along the evolutionary journey which brought us to our present stature, we were like him. For some, as natural history spanned space and time beyond the limits of our imaginations, God, as creator, became increasingly remote, leaving a vacancy which was filled by our primitive. He is the counterpart to Adam, that man made by God, for he is primal man who shed his fur, stood upright, and gradually made himself by his wit, his sexuality, his language, his mistakes, and his drive for knowledge.

Deeply embedded in our consciousness and lore, our primitive serves a wide range of social and religious functions, from gaining social conformity to channeling protest and social criticism. *The New Yorker,* for example, may use images of our primitive in cartoons to remind us of our intellectual and imaginative infancy. *Playboy* may use images of the figure to remind us of our deeply seated sexuality, disguised in sophisticated attire. Our primitive is used to protest the defilement of nature and to influence dietary patterns and economic trends. We find him everywhere, and he will live on in our imaginations and lore.

Upon recognizing the importance and historical background of this character, we can begin to appreciate the order of error committed when we approach any peoples in the world and call them primitive.[1] When we do this we force the peoples we meet to conform to the images and expectations of our primitive; that is, we see them *only* in the terms of our expectations. Although objectivity is impossible and not even desirable, and while our views must always play a vital role in our studies, we must nonetheless do everything we can to try to meet these peoples on their own terms.

An insidious form of prejudice is borne even in the term primitive. Let us look at it more closely. It is a relative term, as are the terms *large* and *small*. A thing or a people is primitive only in relation to some other thing or some other people; and herein lies one of the greatest of our errors in applying the term *primitive* to actual peoples and cultures. We can see this in a view widely held since the late nineteenth century. Under the immense impact of the idea of evolution, many turned to the task of describing the evolution of cultural forms. To them, the cultures and religions of Western civilization were at the apex and they proceeded to align other cultures in a temporal chain according to their level of development. The cultures placed at an earlier stage were, according to this proposition, inferior to our own, and this seemed obvious at least in terms of material culture. But according to this reasoning contemporary cultures that somehow resemble earlier stages of cultural development, particularly in material and technological areas, were located at an earlier and hence lower stage of development. In relative terms these ''other'' cultures were described as ''primitive'' and by a host of associated terms, such as savage, uncivilized, simple, and archaic. This effort doubtless added much to the creation of our figure, the primitive, but we have only begun to understand that its results were largely formed to meet the needs of our own history. We have only begun to comprehend the inaccuracy of our understanding of these other peoples, and as a consequence, the injustice of the way in which we have treated them.

We can see the nature of this error when we compare the images of the ''caveman'' and the ''natives'' as previously described. Notice that we have different temporal associations with the two sets of images. We associate the caveman with the remote past, when man was little more than ape; and we consider the natives to be contemporary to us, yet remote from us in space. Still we consign both to the same stage of development when we refer to them by the common term primitive. Although the error of equating early man with contemporary peoples is obvious, it has nonetheless been common practice. For example, upon the recent meeting (interestingly we call it ''discovery'') of the Tasadays in the Phillipines, it was promptly announced that they are a ''Stone Age people.'' Clearer thinking tells us that there are no Stone Age peoples apart from the Stone Age. There may be contemporary peoples who have a technology similar to that of peoples living in the Stone Age. When we consign our contem-

---

[1] For a collection of articles on the concept of the primitive see Ashley Montagu, ed., *The Concept of the Primitive* (New York: The Free Press, 1968). For critical comment on the scholarly approach that has been taken in the study of the religions of nonliterate peoples from the perspective of religious studies, see Mircea Eliade, *Australian Religion: An Introduction* (Ithaca, N.Y.: Cornell University Press, 1973), pp. xi-xxi.

poraries to an era millennia ago, we do not permit them to have experienced a history equal in length to our own; we assign to them an accompanying inferiority; we force them to serve the enhancement of our own image of ourselves; and we create such a temporal abyss between ourselves and them that we can scarcely begin to enter into a relationship with them. Also in doing this we reveal that above all we value the advancement of material culture.

As we prepare to meet these "other peoples" it is essential for us to understand that the term *primitive* came about in Western history as a product of our looking to the peoples in the forests which surrounded Western civilization in order to set off, as by foil, how sophisticated and advanced we felt we had become. But we have looked into the forest dimly, for we have seen only what we have wanted to see. Amazingly, we have yet to distinguish clearly between our images and the peoples we think we have been seeing.

It follows that when we think in terms like "primitive religion" or "the religions of primitive peoples," we are likely to be conditioned to think of a stage in the evolution of religion prior to the present, prior to our own, and therefore inferior.[2]

What we must face initially in this study is the fact that we have probably inherited a set of images and attitudes which, if taken with us in the endeavor to understand the religions of these "other peoples," will introduce inaccuracies and will mislead us, perhaps without our even knowing it. But with this knowledge, we will more likely succeed in understanding the religions of these "other peoples" because we may avoid prejudicing our view by the images we have of our primitive.

NONLITERACY

Having said this much we are now faced with the problem of what to call these "other peoples" so that we may refer to them without confusion. If we listen to how they have identified themselves, especially when distinguishing themselves from us we may find a clue.

In the late nineteenth century, Frank Hamilton Cushing went to live with the Zuni, a North American tribe residing in present day New Mexico. The Zuni still remember Cushing in their poetry. One poem recalls the occasion when they initiated him into their Bow Priesthood.

> *Once they made a White man into a Priest of the Bow*
> *he was out there with other Bow Priests*
> *he had black stripes on his body*
> *the others said their prayers from their hearts*
> *but he read his from a piece of paper.*

---

[2] For a presentation of the major theories of religion which have dictated the study of the religions of nonliterate cultures, see E. E. Evans-Pritchard, *Theories of Primitive Religion* (London: Oxford University Press, 1965).

The term for written page in Zuni language, as Dennis Tedlock noted, is literally "that which is striped." As a Bow Priest, with his white body covered with black stripes, Cushing was a walking page of writing.[3] Their poetic sophistication adds strength to the distinction the Zuni are making between themselves as a people of the spoken word in contrast to Cushing, an outsider, who is identified as a heartless walking page of writing.

A member of the Carrier tribe of British Columbia compared his people's knowledge of the animals to that held by the "white man." He said, "The white man writes everything down in a book so that it will not be forgotten; but our ancestors married the animals, learned all their ways, and passed on the knowledge from one generation to another."[4]

In his eloquent address, "The Man Made of Words," N. Scott Momaday convincingly shows that many Native American peoples consider the spoken word as supremely creative. We can see this idea expressed when the Uitoto, a forest-dwelling people in southeastern Columbia, say, "In the beginning, the word gave origin to the father."[5]

This creative power of the spoken word is common in African cultures as well. Amadou Hampâte Bâ, a West African scholar, said that "in oral civilization the word engages man, the word *is* man. The word is creative. It maintains man in his own nature."[6] In much of Africa the spoken word has attained the stature we attribute to the most sacred writings.

In Australia, New Guinea, and wherever one finds these "other peoples," we commonly observe the spoken word has special significance; we note the recognition of the spoken word as inseparable from way of life and identity; and we see that these peoples often point to the differences between the spoken and written word to distinguish themselves from us.

This phenomenon suggests that the emphasis upon orality and the absence of alphabetic writing systems, which we may identify by the term *nonliteracy,* is at least one major clearly identifiable feature which helps distinguish these peoples. Although it has certain problems which I will discuss, I believe it is a useful term in that it points us in the direction of seeing the religions of these peoples as cultural activities involving speech and visual symbols which are creative in a most vital way.

As to its problems, *nonliteracy,* like primitive, is a relative term, but it makes clear the category in which the relation is being drawn. Unfortunately, we

[3] Dennis Tedlock, "Verbal Art," *Handbook of North American Indians,* ed. William C. Sturtevant (Washington, D.C.: Smithsonian Institution, in press), Chapter 50, Vol. 1.

[4] Diamond Jenness, "The Carrier Indians of the Bulkley River," Bulletin No. 133, *Bureau of American Ethnology,* Washington, D.C., 1943, p. 540.

[5] Margot Astrov, *American Indian Prose and Poetry: An Anthology* (New York: The John Day Co., 1972), p. 20.

[6] Amadou Hampâte Bâ, *Aspects de la Civilisation Africaine* (Paris: Présence Africain, 1972). Quoted in Daniel Whitman, "Africa and the Word," trans. Daniel Whitman, *Parabola,* Vol. II, No. 2 (1977), 66–67. See Whitman for a number of other African examples.

must state the condition negatively; that is, nonliteracy refers to those people who do *not* write their language. But the positive statement, *oral peoples,* is neither sufficient nor distinctive, since peoples who write their languages also have extensive oral aspects of religion and culture, and since we are pointing to more than speech. The term *nonliteracy* should not carry the prejudicial notion of inferiority or the ambiguity of *primitive,* but it must be made clear that we do not mean *preliterate.* There is no evidence that literacy is a necessary condition for enjoying the fullness of life or receiving the meaning which religion can give. It is not a stage of development that need yield to one distinguished by literacy. Further, we do not mean *illiterate, unlearned,* or *unintelligent.* As it will become increasingly clear, none of these is distinctive of nonliterate peoples.

In the adoption of the term *nonliterate peoples* my primary concern is not to distinguish a type of culture so much as to identify a mode or feature which is most common and important to those cultures, ancient and contemporary, whose people live in small communities, have subsistence economies, and who do not write their languages. The term nonliteracy points to a set of important factors which distinctly shape the character of this type of culture, yet it is not entirely adequate as a term to identify a culture type. On the one hand, there are other features which are perhaps equally important in shaping the character of these cultures, like their scale or self-sufficiency; and, on the other hand, all cultures are doubtless shaped to some extent by the very factors we identify with nonliteracy.

To focus on nonliteracy then is not the only way to distinguish these peoples and to attempt to understand their religions, but it does give us a perspective from which to think about and to interpret the data we have. If we are careful it is not a highly prejudiced perspective and it permits us to recognize our genuine differences as well as our vital similarities.

Whether or not one's language can be written does not indicate a great and clearly defined division between types of religion and culture, but it is not difficult to see that it greatly shapes and affects the way in which culture is transmitted, its size and extent, the legal and economic systems, and a whole range of factors that are related to religion. The presence of writing in a religious tradition can be greatly clarifying, opening numerous choices and serving a host of positive functions. Most of the study of religious traditions in modern scholarship has centered upon the translation of sacred writings and the extension of the history of the interpretations and understandings of these writings. The longer the history of a tradition, the more extensive the body of written materials.

In cultures without writing, there are no canons of sacred scripture, no libraries of interpretive writings, no written histories of thought. It is not that sacred religious teachings and related intellectual thought are lacking, but that they are borne in oral traditions and in an array of cultural forms from architecture to music. All knowledge in a nonliterate culture is contained in the memories of its living members. Since the wisdom of the entire history of culture and its intellectual thought must be held in this way, the language of oral tradi-

tion and the visual forms of ritual, art, and culture are highly symbolic and pregnant with meaning.

If we are to understand the religions of nonliterate peoples there are no
convenient dividing lines between the religious and the other domains of culture.
One can scarcely imagine how to approach the religions of nonliterate peoples
without interpreting the religious significance of such diverse forms as stories,
songs, poetry, ritual drama, dance, art, and architecture. Religion is a part of
almost all aspects of life, from activities providing daily sustenance to the most
common utensils. Although it is quite clear that this factor is perhaps no less true
of the religions of cultures with writing, we have usually made the choice to
study primarily the written texts and to ignore the religious values of broader
cultural forms. Yet religion is a cultural phenomenon, thus the study of the
religions of nonliterate peoples, which can only be approached from a cultural
perspective, is not simply a curiosity unrelated to the rest of the history of
religions. It is a relevant and important study because, while it illuminates the
religions of a particular type of culture, it also contributes to our understanding
of aspects of religion which, although present and essential in every religious
culture, have not been given adequate attention.

If we consider the history of humankind, we recognize that we may include
as nonliterate all the peoples prior to the advent of written languages, approximately five thousand years ago, and since then, most of the tribal peoples living
throughout the world. (The last few centuries have witnessed the great expan-
sion of our knowledge of the nonliterate peoples of the world.) We think of the
indigenous peoples of Africa, the Americas, Australia, the Pacific Islands,
Siberia, and Indonesia. Then, of course, on the basis of archaeological evidence
we have some knowledge of the nonliterate peoples of prehistory from the
Paleolithic era. Given these vast numbers of peoples, each with a history, each
with a way of life and religion distinct from all other peoples, we must ask how
we can lump them together under a single heading in order to study their
religions. Numerous volumes have been written about many of these peoples,
describing their ways of life and their religions. For the Hopi, a small Pueblo
tribe in the American Southwest, there is a published bibliography containing
three thousand items. With thousands of cultures equally as significant and complex as the Hopi we can only hope to present a modest introduction to this vast
area of study.

Throughout the book examples selected from a wide range of nonliterate
cultures will be presented in as full a manner as possible in limited space. These
will be interpreted as particular religious events, but the examples and their interpretations will commonly become the base for more general discussions.
Hence the primary interest will be to establish a stance from which to understand the religions of nonliterate peoples, and this will be done through the
discussion of select examples and not in the presentation of a complete summary
or introduction to the known facts. The thread of continuity will largely stem
from the set of factors we will associate with nonliteracy.

Nonliteracy greatly shapes conceptions of time and space, of history and geography. This fundamental consideration will be the subject of Chapter 2. By investigating orientations in time and space we may acquire the basic vocabulary that will help us to understand more fully the nature of nonliterate traditions.

Since there are no written texts produced by members of these cultures, our sources are often objects and acts which we usually identify as art. In Chapter 3 we will attempt to learn how to "read the meaning" of these objects and actions; we will consider whether or not they should be thought of as art; and we will ask how aesthetics relate to religion.

The expression of the religions of nonliterate peoples is shaped by the primary modes of sustenance. If, for example, a people are primarily hunters their symbolic expressions of religious belief are usually couched in terms associated with animals and the hunting relationship. In Chapter 4 we will consider this dimension of the religions of nonliterate peoples.

The richest forms in which the religions of nonliterate peoples are expressed and brought into action in culture are the oral traditions and rituals. These are very complex and widely ranging subjects. The character and significance of these forms will be the subjects of Chapters 5 and 6. These chapters are heavily dependent upon the earlier chapters, which provide the terminology and point of view for the consideration of these cultural forms.

It has been widely observed that nonliterate peoples are rapidly disappearing from the earth as modernity is introduced through colonization, missionization, and the development of worldwide communications, a process which has been accelerating during the last several centuries. Thus it is important to present the religions of nonliterate peoples, not as isolated and free from the influences of literate peoples, but in the terms of their confrontation with and responses to these influences. Although the meeting with literate cultures will color examples presented throughout the book, religious forms which have been generated by this particular situation will be the subject of Chapter 7. In Chapter 8, a brief summary and statement of conclusion will bring the topic to its close.

2

a place on which to stand:[1] orientations in time and space

The Navajo bless a new home before they live in it. The ceremony includes this song:

> ho-wo-o-ho, ho-wo-o-ho
> *At a holy home place I indeed arrived,* holaghai.
> *At his home of Earth I indeed arrived,*
> *At his home of vegetation I indeed arrived,*
> *At his home of all kinds of fabrics I indeed arrived,*
> *Now at his home of long life, now happiness I indeed*
>   *arrived,* holaghai,
> *At his home of Mountain Woman I indeed arrived,*
> *At his home of Rain Mountain I indeed arrived,*
> *At his home of jewels I indeed arrived,*
> *Now at his home of long life, now happiness I indeed*
>   *arrived,* holaghai,
> *At his home of Water Woman I indeed arrived,*
> *At his home of collected waters I indeed arrived,*
> *Now at his home of long life, now happiness I indeed*
>   *arrived,* holaghai,

---

[1] This title is taken from Jonathan Z. Smith, "The Influence of Symbols upon Social Change: A Place on Which to Stand," in *The Roots of Ritual,* ed. James D. Shaughnessy (Grand Rapids, Mich.: William B. Eerdmans Publishing Company, 1973), pp. 121–44.

At his home of Corn Woman I indeed arrived,
At his home of pollen I indeed arrived,
Now at his home of long life, now happiness I indeed
arrived, at a holy place I indeed have arrived.[2]

Singing this song a deity named Talking God announces his arrival at the original Navajo home constructed according to his instructions in the era when the Navajo world was made. The supporting pillars of the Navajo home are named and identified with the deities that support the whole cosmos—Earth, Mountain Woman, Water Woman, and Corn Woman. When Navajos sing this song Talking God's presence blesses their home, which is built in the very shape of the Navajo world.

The Ndembu of Zambia recognize a number of different categories of blood: the blood of animals, the blood of parturition, the blood of menstruation, the blood of murder, and the blood of witchcraft or sorcery. When investigating the significance of color symbolism among the Ndembu, Victor Turner found that the symbolism of red is tied to its relationship to blood. "Red things have power; blood is power, for a man, an animal, an insect, or a bird must have blood, or it will die. Wooden figurines have no blood and hence cannot breathe, speak, sing, laugh, or chat together—they are only carvings in wood. But if the figurines used by sorcerers are given blood, they can move about and kill people."[3]

FIGURE 2.1. Navajo hogan.

[2] By permission from *Blessingway: With Three Versions of the Myth Recorded and Translated from the Navajo by Father Berard Haile, O.F.M.,* by Leland C. Wyman (Tucson: University of Arizona Press, copyright 1970), pp. 118-19.

[3] Victor Turner, *The Forest of Symbols* (Ithaca, N.Y.: Cornell University Press, 1967), pp. 70-71.

During their month-long nubility rites, called Chisungu, the Bantu girls of Zambia are housed in a special hut. Many of the rites take place in this special place or in the bush.[4]

The Quiché of Santiago El Palmar believe in witches who have the power to transform themselves into animals and birds to perform their evil tasks. Commonly in animal form they take sexual advantage of sleeping women, combining the crimes of bestiality and rape. The Quiché identify signs of witches by animals or birds who behave in a peculiar manner or are particularly ugly and by people who have bloodshot eyes, large and protruding canine teeth, or a habit of sleeping rather than working during the daytime.[5]

These several cases may appear to have little in common, but they have been selected to introduce a matter that is crucial to our appreciation and understanding of the religions of nonliterate peoples. One commonality of these examples is that they all reflect a concern for *place*, for where one stands with respect to time and space, and we can see that this concern has religious significance. The Navajo songs are part of the ritual to make a physical structure into a sacred place. The Ndembu symbolism of red is bound up with blood, but the significance of blood, in turn, is dependent upon where it is, upon its place. Its meaning is ambivalent apart from place. The Bantu girls' puberty rite identifies a change in social and sexual status with a change in physical place. The Quiché identify a witch by his or her contradiction of expectations concerning place. To be out of place, in either space or time, indicates for the Quiché a potential witch.

Our initial inclination may be to approach the study of the religions of nonliterate peoples in terms of their institutions and teachings, but as will become increasingly clear, this approach may not direct us toward the fullest understanding of the way in which religion is experienced and serves felt human needs. As an alternative I want to take seriously the concern for place which is apparent in the previous examples and to develop from this concern an approach to our study of these religions. Wherever it is found religion serves to create and define human orientations and meaning-laden boundaries, and it does so in the concrete terms of time and space. To focus our study on those most fundamental orientations may reveal to us the way in which a people view their world. It gives us the principles of order within a religious world view, but it also permits us to appreciate such things as the religious role of pollution, taboo, witchcraft, and sorcery, which in their way, help to define the character of place.[6]

Since this concern with place is not confined to the religions of nonliterate peoples, it consequently provides the much needed language that permits us to

[4] Audrey I. Richards, *Chisungu* (London: Faber and Faber, 1956).

[5] Benson Saler, "Nagual, Witch, and Sorcerer in a Quiché Village," in *Magic, Witchcraft, and Curing*, ed. John Middleton (Austin: University of Texas Press, 1967), pp. 79–80.

[6] See particularly the works by Jonathan Z. Smith, Mircea Eliade, Claude Levi-Strauss, and Mary Douglas in the "Bibliography."

talk about their religions in terms both we and our subjects are more likely to understand. Furthermore, this kind of approach is important since the materials—objects and actions—we must interpret are highly symbolic and gain their religious values by the way they define, occupy, and manipulate time and space.

The song which blesses the Navajo home and the home being blessed are not Navajo religious institutions in terms familiar to us, nor do we recognize these as being religious teachings. But in the house blessing the Navajo people reveal something very central to their religious tradition. In their view Navajo homes are not ordinary structures of merely utilitarian value; their homes replicate the very shape of the cosmos, that is, of the entire Navajo world. In this sense every home is symbolic in that it speaks of something far greater than what is physically apparent. And it is through their manipulation of time and space, in this case the construction of their houses to replicate a primordial form, that the Navajos can make this religious statement.

Our success in this approach will depend upon how well we are able to interpret the religious beliefs and values which are reflected in the temporal and spatial dimensions of the symbolic objects and actions through which people discern and effect meaning in their lives. In order both to begin our introduction to the religions of nonliterate peoples and to prepare us for the task of interpreting their religious symbols, we will devote this chapter to the fundamental matters of time and space.

TIME

Many cultures do not have a word that even roughly approximates our word *time,* whereas others have a number of terms to distinguish the varieties of temporal experiences which we identify by a single term. While the abstraction and conceptualization of something called time is not common to all peoples, time, from our perspective, is one of the principal dimensions, along with space, in which human beings orient themselves within reality.

Philosophers and physicists have shown us that there is no such ''thing'' as time. Time is not something empirically given in the world to be laid out and measured. At first this may seem strange, but we must comprehend this idea if we are to be able to understand the freedom human beings have to create their own experiences of time by the ways in which they structure their lives. Seeing time as a human creation, we may appreciate temporal orientation as symbolic of the way a people understand the nature of human existence. Thus, uses of time, orientations within time, structured processes are data valuable to us in our efforts to understand another religion for they are religiously symbolic.

Moving beyond this abstract level of the subject we will now outline in concrete terms several domains of culture in which temporal experiences may be symbolically expressed. These domains are identified with ecology or occupation, social structure, history, stories of origin, and ritual. The complex, sometimes paradoxical, character of time is expressed in these forms. We will then present a specific cultural example for discussion.

ECOLOGY AND OCCUPATION.[7] For relatively short periods, time is reckoned with respect to human activities related to *ecology* and *occupation:* chores, meals, and sleep; and hunting, planting, and harvesting. These activities identify times, and these times correspond to natural cycles of day and night and seasonal changes. These temporal experiences are likely to be associated with repetition and oscillation, as a cycle of events with a regular succession.

Ecological divisions of time may vary markedly from culture to culture. The Nuer, a cattle-herding people of southern Sudan, for example, divide the year into two seasons corresponding only approximately to a season of rain, during which they live in villages, and a dry season spent in camps by streams and lakes. Notably the Nuer do not refer to these divisions as periods of time but rather as predominant social activities. They would say "I am going to *tot* in such and such a place," wherein *tot* refers to the social and economic activities of the wet season. In contrast to the Nuer are the Maenge, a taro-growing people of Melanesia, who, although making a distinction between dry season and wet season, have no sense of a polarized seasonal cycle, but rather reckon a sequence of flowing, loosely demarked seasons. Time reckoning is based very flexibly on a series of flowering plants correlated with lunar cycles. Time is reckoned by a kind of olfactory system in which one can smell what time it is.[8]

SOCIAL STRUCTURE. Societies commonly identify various stages of life and age groupings, such as youth, adolescence, maturity, and old age, as well as generations and lineages. Thus, the *social structure* embodies a temporal order. Here time is more likely to be experienced as a duration, that is, the time of a certain ancestor or the time of youth, characterized as irreversible and nonrepetitive. This way of designating time is reflected in our common phrases like "in my grandfather's time" and "before I was married." Still in some nonliterate cultures like the Guahibo in Brazil, where there is little concern with geneology and where social structure does not greatly differentiate members of the culture, social stratification has little association with temporal references.[9]

HISTORY. In contrast to the position commonly held, nonliterate peoples are not without a sense of *history.* Surely all cultures recognize that their present

---

[7] Anthropological studies of time in nonliterate cultures have been almost exclusively interested in how time is reckoned and the foundational study in this area is that of E. E. Evans-Pritchard, "Nuer Time Reckoning," *Africa,* Vol. 12 (1939), 189–216. Evans-Pritchard found that time reckoning was related to ecological activities—planting, harvesting, fishing—and to the structure of society—the age groupings and ordering principles of generations and lineages.

[8] Michel Panoff, "The Notion of Time Among the Maenge People of New Britain," *Ethnology,* Vol. 8 (1969), 153–66.

[9] Robert V. Morey, "Guahibo Time-Reckoning," *Anthropological Quarterly,* Vol. 44 (1971), 22–36.

conditions have been shaped by significant historical events, such as floods, wars, and epidemics, or events which are sufficiently unusual, such as eclipses or the extraordinary feats of individuals. This domain of history may extend the scope and reference points of temporal orientation significantly beyond the lifetime of the living and their own experiences.

Tuber cultivators in New Guinea periodically move their village location as the surrounding land becomes exhausted. Temporal references spanning considerable periods are commonly reckoned by indexing events to village and garden locations. These historical reckonings may endure well beyond the lifetime of those who experienced the events. In parts of North America, native peoples still refer to "the night the stars fell," a spectacular meteor shower in 1832. The Kwakiutl of the Pacific Northwest maintain geneologies extending many generations. Among nonliterate peoples we will not find history written or ordered upon a numbered chronological scale, but we shouldn't dismiss its existence. History is a temporal experience characterized by nonrepetition and duration.

STORIES OF ORIGIN. One of the most distinctive ways in which nonliterate peoples place themselves in reality is by accounting for their origins. In *stories of origin,* orientation is achieved by indicating how things were sanctioned to be "in the beginning." Although these stories are always set in primordial time, we should not read them as history, that is, as referring to events of some specific length of time before the present. Primordial time is unlike human time, and although it has an a priori relationship to the present world, suggesting its pastness, it is held to be central to the meaning of the present reality; events "in the beginning" constitute the unquestioned authoritative base for the present. The placement of events "in the beginning" is the utilization of temporal symbolism to establish primacy, and because of this temporal primacy these stories exercise great influence upon the lifeways of the people.

RITUAL. Repetition is an essential characteristic of the nature of *ritual.* Like the cycles in nature, the occurrence and form of ritual are dependable, and this dependability is manifest within the temporal dimension. Rooted in tradition, even in the acts of the gods and ancestors, ritual manipulates the human experience and valuation of time by its repetitions and reenactments which constitute ways of life. It seves not only to reckon time but also to create it. That is, time is not simply told by the occurrence of a festival or ritual event; the enactment of ritual actually serves to initiate, to delimit, to make a new time.

Again to recall a familiar example to illustrate, if we refer to the time of our marriage, we are not referring to a time delineated by a calendar; we are referring to a period of time set off by the transformative power of a ritual event. Marriage does not occur without ceremony, nor do many significant events in the cultures of nonliterate peoples, as we will discuss in Chapter 6. Ritual performances commonly serve to formally delimit periods of time. They transform single persons into a married unit, a youth into an adult, a dormant season into an agricultural season. We can reckon time from these events, as in the length of one's married life, but in doing so we must understand that the ritual of marriage actually initiated that time.

These five areas are interrelated and tend to overlap in varied and complex ways. As here ordered each expands in scope the domain of temporal concern. The area of *ecology* and *occupation* is narrowest, and the *origin story* and *ritual* areas are broadest. Human actions may engage any or all of these levels. For example, the activity of planting crops may reckon planting time, a season or time of the year. It may also be an activity modeled upon the stories of gods and ancestors who gave seeds to humans and revealed the manner of planting. Planting may be associated with certain cultural domains, such as women and earth. It may be accompanied by or performed as ritual, serving to expand greatly its felt significance.

We can appreciate the complexity of the symbolism of time and how it is engaged at each of these domains in interrelated and overlapping ways by the examination of an extended example from one culture. Since much has been written about Hopi conceptions of time, let us consider them. Benjamin Lee Whorf's studies of Hopi language created a still reverberating series of shock waves. Whorf found that Hopi language does not have tense in the ordinary sense of having verb forms which distinguish past, present, and future.[10] This observation—linked with a hypothesis of linguistic determinism proposed by Whorf and Edward Sapir, which proclaimed that language determines one's view of reality—suggested that the Hopi must experience time in ways strangely different from us. Some have even taken this view to the full extent of supposing that the Hopi do not perceive time at all but live in a mystical timeless world. Upon reviewing Hopi culture in terms of the five domains we have discussed we get quite a different picture.

The Hopi are a small-scale maize (corn)-growing people who have lived at the southern tip of Black Mesa in northern Arizona for centuries. The Hopi village, Oraibi, is probably the longest continuously inhabited place in North America today. This high desert area is very dry, yet there is dependable summer rainfall which is essential for the maize. The Hopi have a precise calendar of major ceremonials and agricultural activities corresponding with solar and lunar movements. A sun-watcher in each Hopi village examines the eastern horizon to note where the sun rises. By the place of the sun on the horizon he can reckon the progress of the sun's movements through the year, information ecologically vital to Hopi people. Major ceremonials correspond with the solstices, marking the bifurcation in the annual calendar. Since many Hopi now commute by automobile some distance for employment, and some stay away throughout the work week, the calendar is adjusted slightly so that major ceremonial and

---

[10] John B. Carroll, ed., *Language, Thought, and Reality: Selected Writings of Benjamin Lee Whorf* (New York: John Wiley & Sons, Inc., 1956).

agricultural occasions occur on weekends. The *ecological* and *occupational* level of time reckoning is characterized as highly regular, cyclic, and repetitive.

The complicated Hopi *social structure* is ordered about principles which assure growth in knowledge and wisdom throughout life. An individual's life is seen not as a cycle but as a road ideologically oriented in space from west to east. The road begins with conception, and there are formal moments of passage which mark and effect one's steps along its entire length. Upon physical birth, the mother and baby remain in the mother's clan house and away from the sun for twenty days before the baby is born into the community and world. On the morning of the twentieth day the baby is presented to the rising sun and given names by its father's clanswomen. These are but the first steps of the long road leading through life which prepares one for a destiny as a kachina (messenger spirit between physical and spiritual domains) or a cloud spirit (spiritual beings of rain, and hence life, to the Hopi people).

Age level and generation serve to place each individual among all Hopi, as reflected even in kinship terms, which index seniority. Responsibility, ownership, authority, knowledge, prestige, religious duties, and many other things are keyed to one's place along the road of life. Clans, lineages, and even villages are responsible for specific ceremonial and occupational tasks and these are determined in accordance with the annual cycle of ceremonies and ecological activities. Clearly, social structure, occupational activity, and temporal orientations are interdependent.

In their oral traditions the Hopi retain a long and rich *history*; although until very recently, and even now only in minor ways, they have not associated historical events with a numbered chronology. Many events which are broadly known can be placed in a relative time sequence extending well beyond the lifetimes of living Hopi. Earliest are the migrations which followed their creation and emergence onto the earth surface. Although the historical detail of these migrations cannot be independently verified, it can be demonstrated that the Hopi place these stories within an historical time frame.

There are many stories about the Spanish who have occasionally visited the Hopi since the early sixteenth century. Among these are the stories of the Pueblo Revolt in 1680, when the Spanish were expelled from the Southwest. The Tewa village of Hano was founded at Hopi when the Spanish reconquered the Rio Grande River area in New Mexico. This is a lively subject of Hopi oral history. The destruction of the Christianized village of Awatovi around 1700 is remembered and has been the subject and inspiration of much contemporary art. A host of stories about relations with other Native American peoples, especially the Navajo, whose lands surround Hopiland, are historically rich. Abundant are the stories about specific Hopi historical incidents long past but transmitted from generation to generation not as legends or tales which took place "once upon a time," but as stories placed historically in terms of specific generations. Whereas there is no history written in Hopi language, it is clear that the Hopi are concerned with history and that it is not only rich but also long.

The Hopi *stories of origin* tell of the journey of the Hopi's predecessors through lower worlds to gain residence on the present earth surface. From the point of view of being placed before all other events these stories set the scene in which Hopi history occurs. But the origin stories, and to an extent even the migration stories, which conclude with the founding of the clans and villages at Hopi, are different from other historical events in a very important sense. These stories present a perfect, or sacred, history because they tell the acts of the creators done in the time when Hopi people and the deities all lived together. These stories present the structure of the universe and the principles upon which it works. These stories establish the basis for all present cultural forms and practices and for interpreting the significance of all of Hopi history. These origin stories have their own histories; that is, they may change slightly over time, by digesting existential events, but it is the distinction of their form to describe the events of "the beginning." And since these events establish the very principles for Hopi life, they are more immediately and vitally relevant than Hopi history. Instead of being placed at the most remote past, origin stories provide an ambience surrounding the present, giving it form and meaning. They define the most fundamental aspects of present reality.

Although the sun is carefully watched to determine the timing of occupational and ceremonial events, it is the responsibility of the Hopi to perform the *ritual* acts that direct the sun along its course. From one Hopi perspective, the sun is perceived as a deity, and it is through ritual that the Hopi interact with the sun as god, an interaction essential to Hopi life. The solstice rites are performed in order to turn the sun back in its course so that the seasons may proceed. Indeed, there is a whole cycle of ritual acts which do not simply celebrate moments in a calendar but actually create the time periods of the calendar. They serve to conclude one period of time and its corresponding activities and moods and initiate a new time and its set of moods and activities. A sequence of rituals enact the passage from life stage to life stage carrying individuals along their life roads.

It is clear that temporal symbolism is basic to Hopi orientation within reality. As it has been our purpose to illustrate, we can see that an analysis of Hopi temporal symbols helps us to understand the basic character of Hopi religion. Every Hopi sees that his or her place in the world is defined and given meaning by the intersection of many temporal planes. For the Hopi, time is not some external thing to be reckoned, nor is it some primordial sequence to be endlessly repeated. Time is not a thing at all, but rather a process which is inseparable from the human processes of living creatively and meaningfully. Sunwatching is not clock-watching; it is observing the manifestation of life processes resulting from the divine-human acts of creation which constantly engage the Hopi in their occupations and rituals.[11]

But what of the lack of tense in the Hopi language? Our review of Hopi

---

[11] For basic information about Hopi conceptions of time see Richard M. Bradfield, *A Natural History of Associations,* Vol. II (London: Duckworth, 1973), pp. 1–342.

temporal planes has shown us that it is not the pastness or presentness that makes an action significant at all, but rather how it is viewed, what is its experiential quality, how it informs the character of the place on which one stands. Clearly the Hopi can distinguish between past, present, and future events as well as can any, but their language reflects that they evaluate temporal experience in different terms.

The temporal symbolism of nonliterate peoples is not radically different in kind from that of literate peoples. Temporal symbolism is as varied and complex as are the systems of religious thought and action they express. Yet certain symbolic forms and aspects of the temporal orientations common among nonliterate peoples may be linked with their lack of writing. For example, time orientations that are associated with an ever-accumulating record of the past held more or less changeless by a permanent record are difficult without writing and do not exist in nonliterate cultures. History is not absent in nonliterate cultures, but since it is an oral tradition it tends to merge with legend and tale. The highly symbolic forms of stories of origin and ritual tend to be central in nonliterate cultures because they help to facilitate the retention in the memory of living people the whole of the knowledge and experience in forms that digest existential experience and expel the irrelevant.

SPACE

The Achilpa are an Arunta tribe of gatherers and small game hunters in Australia. According to their stories, their world was created by a deity named Numbakula. He not only made the world; he also created the ancestors of the people and lived with them for a time in order to establish their way of life. When he had finished his work of creation, Numbakula made a pole from the trunk of a gum tree. Upon anointing the pole with blood, he climbed it and disappeared into the sky.

The Achilpa kept the pole as their most sacred possession and it stood at the center of their lives, reminding them of the ways that had been established for them by Numbakula. They used the pole to direct their nomadic movements. When they were ready to move to a new location, they consulted the pole and moved in the direction in which it leaned. It was always taken with them and carefully protected.

Baldwin Spencer and F. J. Gillen, who lived among the Achilpa for a time, described what happened once when the sacred pole was broken. The people were very disturbed and confused and seemed to wander about aimlessly for a time until finally they all lay down on the ground to await the death they thought was to come.[12]

---

[12] Baldwin Spencer and F. J. Gillen, *The Arunta*, Vol. I (London: Macmillan & Co., Ltd., 1927), p. 388.

FIGURE 2.2. Pole ascended during fire ceremony (Australia). (Courtesy of the American Museum of Natural History.)

We may think this pole-related action strange, but it is not an uncommon kind of act in the history of religions. Wherever human beings have been, they have made their mark upon the landscape, even by the temporary erection of a pole. Often this mark does not last long, but sometimes it does. The cave paintings in France, which date from the Paleolithic era, are an example of very enduring marks, as are the petroglyphs that appear on rock walls the world over. The markings to which I refer are not insignificant doodles or graffiti, for they signal an important distinction between animals and human beings; moreover, they signal something of the role of religion. The marks are not reproductions of nature; indeed, they rearrange or reorder nature. What is achieved in this peculiarly human activity? It is no less than the human conferral of meaning on the place upon which one stands. With this mark, one declares that the place on which one stands is meaningful. In this way, humans show that they have a relationship with the world around them; a relationship whose sanction and purpose transcends the mere physical character of the place.

Certainly we can see this in the Australian example, as simple as it is. The Achilpa, by carrying their sacred pole with them and by erecting it wherever they camp, are asserting the meaning and order revealed by the deity Numbakula upon the temporary space in which they live. It is the point from which all their activities gain orientation. It signals the basic distinctions which give them identity and by which they cohere. It is the channel through which they may continue to communicate with Numbakula, who lives in the sky. And through it Numbakula can communicate with the people, telling them, among other things, which way to travel. Even though it moves with them, the pole is the fixed point, the point of origin, the point giving meaning about which their lives are ordered. Seen in this way it is little wonder the Achilpa were so upset and even submitted to death when their sacred pole was broken. Symbolically they were cut off from their deity, from their heritage, from the order and orientation of their world. Without this center, they were symbolically in a state of chaos. Their aimless wandering and submission to death show the degree to which they found the meaning of their lives and livelihoods linked to their sacred pole. It was no ornament, no vacuous symbol, no superstition. It was the center and source of meaning in their whole way of life.

Wherever human beings are found, one of their most primary religious acts is to make some mark upon their landscape by which they can relate to the world in which they live. This mark is made in a host of ways: the construction of an altar or shrine; the building of a house or sanctuary; the naming of mountains or megaliths; the designation of directions by the orientation of ordinary activities; or the establishment of boundaries and perimeters by clearings, walls, or natural features. In so doing human beings are showing that they do not experience all space as having the same value and meaning. If each place were indistinguishable from all others, orientation would be impossible. Mircea Eliade, who has focused a great deal of his work on these designations in space, says that this human act of making a place by designating the special significance of certain places is equivalent to the founding of a world. He says that people must found the world before they can live in it. In making spatial designations like building a house or erecting a pole, the world is constituted, and cosmos emerges from chaos or disorder.[13] We can see that when the Achilpa erect their sacred pole at a new camp it is equivalent to the cosmogonic acts, to the cosmic creation of Numbakula.

Recall the Navajo song at the beginning of this chapter. The supporting pillars of the house are identified with the supporting pillars of the cosmos and with the deities who give life to the earth. The floor is identified with the earth surface, and the dome-shaped structure with the overarching sky. For the Navajo, the building of a house is a religious activity, and it is so because it is equivalent to the act of creating the world. In Navajo culture, the hogan (Navajo home) is the center of life's activities. It always faces east, the direction of the rising sun, and provides orientation for all human activities. Most ceremonial acts are performed in the hogan. We should not be surprised that the Navajo abandon or destroy any hogan in which someone has died, for death in such a life-giving place is the ultimate incongruity. It is a disaster on the order of the broken sacred pole of Achilpa.

In these two examples, we have before us the two dominant features in the designation of space which can be found everywhere: the establishment of a

---

[13] See, for example, Mircea Eliade, "Sacred Space and Making the World Sacred," *The Sacred and the Profane* (New York: Harper & Row, Publishers, Inc., 1959), pp. 20–67.

center and the drawing of peripheral boundaries. In the erection of their sacred pole, the Achilpa founded their world by establishing a center, which functioned as an axis around which the activities of life were oriented. From their point of view it is a world axis as well, and in its cosmological and spiritual functions, it is the point of contact between the earth world of people and the sky world of the deity. We find this kind of designation frequently among nonliterate peoples in a variety of forms. The use of a tree, either as the world axis or as the source from which to cut the pole to serve as the axis, as in the Australian example, is very common since the tree has such a capacity to symbolize life in its unity (trunk) at once with its diversity (branches and fruit).

The center is movable and often even multiple. This is not an example of fallacious primitive logic, but rather it attests to the importance of maintaining orientation in every space and to the appreciation of the efficacy of symbols to do so. The Achilpa carry their center with them even as they travel from area to area. Their meaningful world is thus asserted upon every geography. The Hopi orient themselves to the place of emergence, or *sipapu,* which is ideologically at the center of their world. It is replicated in the floor of every ceremonial chamber (*kiva*) as well as designated as a place in the physical geography located in the canyon of the Little Colorado River in Arizona.

The other dominant way of designating a significant space is by establishing the perimeter or boundaries, as is done in the construction of the Navajo hogan. The effect is to distinguish a space that is associated with one set of qualities and values apart from the peripheral space, which is associated with a contrasting set of qualities and values.

The Bantu-speaking people, who live in the forests of Zaire, also illustrate this way of designating space. Although they live in the heart of the forest, they do not live as a part of the forest world; rather they labor endlessly to clear the trees and bush to create a space in which to plant the crops upon which their lives depend. The clearing is endowed with all the positive values of life—sunlight, health, and happiness—whereas the forest, which is forever encroaching upon their gardens, threatening to squeeze them to death, is bestowed with all the negative qualities of evil, darkness, and witchcraft.

Especially when space is designated by the drawing of perimeters or boundaries, movement between the areas has special significance—which, of course, may vary greatly, depending upon the character of the religious system in which it occurs. For example, whereas the Navajo see the hogan as the center of life and as the place of creation and nourishment, they also believe that one must leave the hogan in order to live in the world. The hogan reflects the form of the Navajo world, but in the domain outside the hogan one engages in interrelationships which, although necessary for life, introduce a potential threat to life. The hogan serves as a kind of womb into which one may return to rest and be nourished or to be ceremonially re-created, but life is lived outside of the home as well; and though it be dangerous and threatening to life, it is necessary. The

Bantu-speaking Negroes, on the other hand, make every effort to avoid entering the forest. They befriend the Pygmy peoples, who live in the forest, in order to obtain the things they need from it, such as meat and ivory.

Doors, thresholds, paths, trails, journeys—all become invested with religious significance when seen as part of the human process of designating space in ways which give meaning to the place on which one stands. Initiates are commonly removed from the village during their initiation rites, a movement in space which suggests both the death of their former stage of life and the danger of being temporarily without a meaningful place. The clan houses of the Pacific northwest coast tribes in North America, such as the Kwakiutl and Tlingit, have huge doors extensively decorated with clan-related spirits. The front walls and doorways are sometimes decorated in the form of a great mouth which devours and swallows its guests, thus protecting them while they are in the container of the house. It is a passage which transforms one into the space of the spirit world. This is analogous to the Kwakiutl notion that the body is the house of the soul. Within these clan houses the people, except for the chief or elder who has quarters behind a special partition, live in a common area. The entryway to the chief's private quarters is decorated so as to represent the vagina of a deity. The chief retires by entering the womb of the clan deity and is born again from her each morning. His importance in sustaining the life of his clansmen is enacted in this way every day.

Ritual can be understood from one perspective as the formal manipulation of space in order to invest it with meaning and thereby to create the world. This ritual function will be seen again and again in Chapter 6, but an example here will help in illustrating the way in which space is used to express and create religious orientations.

The example is a complex ritual practiced by the Ndembu of Zambia, one from a class of women's rituals which deal with temporary barrenness. A woman who has a number of miscarriages or finds it difficult to become pregnant may feel that her problem is caused by the curse of an ancestor whom she has failed to remember with the appropriate gestures. She considers herself to be "caught" by the ancestor's spirit, and in the ritual she attempts to appease the offended spirit in order to regain her reproductive capacities.

First a diviner is procured to determine the specific nature of the affliction, the ancestral spirit involved, and the nature of the spirit's curse. With this information, a doctor who knows the appropriate medicines performs, with the aid of others who have been similarly treated, rituals which amount to the initiation of the woman into a cult of affliction, that is, the order of those who have previously suffered such difficulties and had them treated in a like manner. The curative rite, called *Isoma*, involves the extensive collection and preparation of medicines and a long formal process. It is of special interest to our concern with marking out the landscape that the Ndembu refer to the various elements in the ritual by the term *chijikijilu*, which literally means "landmark" or "blaze" as in

FIGURE 2.3. Isoma ritual: Couple in "hot" hole. (From Victor W. Turner, *The Ritual Process: Structure and Anti-Structure.* Chicago: Aldine Publishing Co., 1969. Used by permission.)

the phrase, "to blaze a trail." The full ritual process has been described by Victor Turner, who witnessed several of these rites.[14]

The selection of the ritual site begins with the location of the stream to which the diviner has traced the curse of the ancestral spirit. At the source of the stream the burrow of a giant rat or ant bear is located. The Ndembu explain that it is the practice of these animals to stop up their burrows after they have dug them, which resembles the woman's barren condition. The burrow becomes the point of orientation for the spatial structuring of the ritual area and the ritual process. When found, an adept (one formerly initiated into the cult) addresses the animal in the hole, calling it the one who kills children and asking that it give fertility back to the woman so that she might bear children again.

With this initial orientation, the ritual area is prepared. Two deep holes are dug, one at the entrance to the animal burrow, "hole of the giant rat," and the other about four feet away along the animal's tunnel, "new hole." The holes and a connecting tunnel become an axis which divides the ritual area. The side to the right when facing the new hole from the burrow's hole is "the right side"; the other, "the left side." Fires are built about ten feet away from the center of this axis on either side. The space around this whole area is cleared of brush,

---

[14] The following description is based on Victor Turner, "Planes of Classification in a Ritual of Life and Death," *The Ritual Process* (Chicago: Aldine Publishing Co., 1969), pp. 1–43.

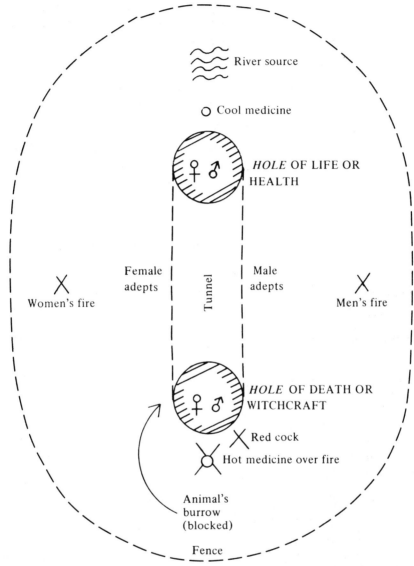

River source

Cool medicine

HOLE OF LIFE OR HEALTH

Female adepts

Tunnel

Male adepts

Women's fire

Men's fire

HOLE OF DEATH OR WITCHCRAFT

Red cock

Hot medicine over fire

Animal's burrow (blocked)

Fence

FIGURE 2.4. Isoma ritual: Schematic representation of spatial symbolism. (Adapted from Victor W. Turner, *The Ritual Process: Structure and Anti-Structure.* Chicago: Aldine Publishing Co., 1969. Used by permission.)

making a small clearing. By considering the names of the areas, the actions of the people when in these areas, the location of medicines and other ritual objects, Turner was able to describe the categories that were evoked and given distinction by the ritual process. These categories correspond with the ordering of space along three axes—a longitudinal, a latitudinal, and an altitudinal—as well as the distinction between the ordered space created in the clearing and the unordered space which surrounds it. The significance of these categories expressed through the symbolic language of space helps us to understand the ritual process and its effects.

The longitudinal axis marks a division between the two holes. The animal burrow entrance, on the one side, is associated with death, witchcraft, and the barrenness suffered by the woman. Near this hole a fire is built, upon which are heated medicines. The heat of this hole is associated with fever, illness, and witchcraft. In contrast, the other hole, the new hole, is associated with life and health. A cool mixture of medicines held in a calabash is placed near this hole. Thus, the distinctions made by this longitudinal axis are as follows: burrow/new hole, death/life, grave/fertility, curse or misfortune/cure, fire/absence of fire, heat/coolness.

The latitudinal axis which bisects the two holes and divides the ritual space between right and left sides, makes a number of other distinctions. Although a fire is built on both sides, there is a clear sexual distinction between them; the woman being treated and the attending women adepts take their places on the left side, the men on the right side.

The altitudinal axis coincides with the ground surface. During the rites, the doctors and adepts remain above the surface of the ground, whereas the woman being treated and her husband enter the holes and move back and forth between the holes by means of the connecting tunnel. They are naked, whereas the adepts are clothed. Hence, according to Turner, the distinctions made along this axis are these: below surface/above surface; initiates/adepts; animals (who dig holes in the ground)/humans; naked/clothed; medicine roots/medicine leaves; in grave/living.

In preparing the ritual space and in enacting the ritual, the Ndembu make their mark on the landscape through these spatial designations made in an otherwise undifferentiated area of bush. In their ritual use of space the Ndembu reflect their belief that the fertility of the woman and her relationship with the ancestral spirit who has caught her in a curse is an affair of the structuring of the world. In this ritual process the Ndembu are able to create the appropriate space and place the suffering woman correctly within that space which at once appeases the ancestor spirit and cures the woman's affliction.

The center of the *Isoma* ritual process amounts to carefully directed movements of the woman and her husband within this designated space. The woman must always stay on the left side, the woman's side. The woman and her husband enter the new hole naked and they are splashed with the cool medicines which identify them with the powers of health and life. They crawl through the tunnel to the burrow's hole, the hot hole, where they are splashed with the hot medicines, which ward off curses, witchcraft, and illness. Crawling back to the cool hole they are splashed again with the cool medicine. All the while the men on the right side and the women on the left side are dancing and singing the songs of the great crisis rites, such as initiation. This movement through the tunnel is repeated a number of times, each beginning and ending at the new hole with a splashing of the cool medicine.

In the ritual process the woman and her husband become, through their orientation within this significant space, physically associated with the categories and distinctions it symbolically defines. But they are more strongly associated with the new hole, the proper sex, fertility, coolness, and curing. At the conclusion of the rite their emergence from the ground is a reentrance into the human world, leaving behind the underground world of the burrowing animals associated with illness and death. It is a new birth into the world from the grave.

CONCLUSION

In this chapter we have found that commonly one's conception of reality and the nature of human existence is inseparable from the character of the place upon which one stands. We have found that for nonliterate peoples the expression of these religious conceptions is not in the form of written theories and dogma, or even in rational discourse, but rather in cultural objects and actions given form by their occupation of time and space. Without documents written by these peoples available for our analysis, there is a heightened importance in our being able to understand these symbolic languages of place. We have seen that time and space are not empirical aspects of reality, simply given to each and every people to be perceived in only one correct way, in only one language. Indeed, it is common among nonliterate peoples not to even have such abstracted noun categories as *time,* as though it were some "thing." Even our familiar distinctions among past, present, and future are not universal; and while we shouldn't conclude therefrom that some people are without the perception and experience of time, we must appreciate that among the peoples of the world there is a rich variety of ways in which to view the world, none necessarily superior or inferior to the others.

There is nothing that distinguishes as unique the place orientations of nonliterate peoples from those of the literate peoples of the world, although there are certain tendencies, which we have noted. By focusing on cultural objects and actions as constituting symbolic languages of place we may become equipped to build bridges, however shaky, between our own views of the world and those of peoples who may seem to be so unlike us.

3

beauty and the drainpipe: art and symbolism in religion

THE SONG OF THE FOREST: IDEAS ABOUT ART AND RELIGION

In the Ituri forest in Zaire, Colin Turnbull lived for a time with the BaMbuti, who are Pygmy people. He shares his experience in a book, *The Forest People*. One of my favorite incidents in the book may help to introduce ideas about the nature of art and symbolism in the religions of nonliterate peoples.

The incident occurs in the context of a ceremonial which takes place over a period of several months. Each night the Pygmy men construct a special communal fire around which they gather to sing and to feast. Their songs are directed toward the forest, which they perceive as their provider, an entity or deity whose presence they feel especially on these occasions. The forest responds to them in beautiful song heard throughout the night from many different places in the forest surrounding the Pygmy camp. The song of the forest is made by the skillful playing of a trumpet. The ceremonial and the trumpet are called by the name *molimo*.

Turnbull had been made fully aware of the sacredness attributed to this nightly ceremony and had felt the Pygmy's reluctance to talk with him about the *molimo*. He had been carefully guarded from seeing the trumpet or knowing much about it.

One evening during the ceremony, Turnbull was happily surprised by an invitation to enter the forest with several young Pygmy men to retrieve the trumpet from its resting place. He was warned that he must keep up with the rapid pace the Pygmies set as they ran along small animal trails through the dense forest. Ater half an hour or so they came to a river, where they paused to wash and purify themselves before they neared the sacred *molimo* trumpet. As they entered a clearing a hush fell over them and several Pygmies went to retrieve the trumpet. Turnbull was filled with the anticipation of seeing what he expected to be an ornately carved bamboo trumpet, the most sacred object of the Pygmy. When the Pygmies returned Turnbull saw them carrying two lengths of drainpipe threaded at the ends, the sacred *molimo* trumpets. The longer, some fifteen feet, was slightly bent in the middle, accidentally caused, no doubt, by being bent around a tree during rapid transit through the forest. To top this, one of the Pygmies approached the trumpet and blew ''a long, raucous raspberry.'' This gesture was received by the others with considerable side slapping and interminable laughter. Turnbull, shocked and disenchanted, asked if these drainpipes didn't constitute a gross sacrilege. But his concerns were met with a counter question: ''What does it matter what the *molimo* is made of? This one makes a great sound, and, besides, it does not rot like wood. It is much trouble to make a wooden one, and then it rots away and you have to make another.''[1]

Moreover, Amabosu, the great singer, soon appeared and demonstrated the potential of the instrument. ''He gently filled the forest with strange sounds—the rumblings and growls of buffalo and leopards, the mighty call of the elephant, the plaintive cooing of the dove. Interspersed with snatches of song, transformed by the trumpet into a sound quite unlike the song of men—richer, softer, more distant and unapproachable.''[2]

If we share Turnbull's shock and disappointment, it is perhaps based on certain ideas we have about the nature of religion and art. We expect that objects of religious importance should be objects of artistic value and should be approached with attitudes of reverence and respect. When confronted by the drainpipe trumpets and the raucous raspberries we find that the Pygmies do not meet our expectations, and we are inclined to dismiss them as a culture simply undeveloped in the areas of art and religion. Many have done so. But we must not dismiss the Pygmies and their *molimo* too quickly, for their response and actions may provide for us a glimpse into the profundity of their perspectives. There is a cluster of ideas suggested in this example. We will lift them up here and then turn to further illustration to develop them.

The event in our example is associated with the religious process in which the Pygmies communicate with the forest as an entity. In what they say and do they show that their religious and aesthetic values are placed on the song produced by the trumpet. They see the physical trumpet as only instrumental. As we would expect, the Pygmies' religious symbols, in this case borne in the form of song, are associated with aesthetic values, but they make it plain to Turnbull,

[1] Colin M. Turnbull, *The Forest People: A Study of the Pygmies of the Congo* (New York: Simon & Schuster, 1961), p. 76.

[2] *Ibid.*, p. 78.

whose attention seems riveted to the trumpets, that objects that are but instrumental in religious processes need not bear these values. The religious object must serve the religious intent unconstrained by aesthetic values. There is no regard for the objects as objects of art. They may be considered utterly commonplace and treated with disregard when out of the sacred context.

Overcoming our initial shock and accepting what the Pygmies say, we may shift our attention from the object to the true bearer of aesthetic and religious values, *sound,* the song of the trumpet. We have identified nonliteracy as a primary distinctive feature of the cultures with which we are concerned, that is, their use of oral and nonverbal rather than literary means by which to bear culture. It should not surprise us to find that sound is a primary medium of the arts and religions of nonliterate cultures.

The Pygmy people have a story about the importance of song. It is called "The Bird with the Most Beautiful Song." It tells of a boy who heard a very beautiful song in the forest. He caught the bird that was singing it and took it home with him. Annoyed at having to feed the bird, the boy's father charged him to get rid of his pet. With persistent pleading, the boy kept the bird for several days. But finally the father took the bird from the boy and dismissed him. "When his son had left, the father killed the Bird, the Bird with the Most Beautiful Song in the Forest, and with the Bird he killed the Song, and with the Song he killed himself and he dropped dead, completely dead, dead forever."[3]

The most beautiful song of the forest is identified with the forest and subsequently with all life within the forest. When the song ceases, the forest does not live. When the forest is dead, it cannot give life to those who live within it.

These Pygmy views may also suggest to us that art is inseparable from religious processes, but that these processes are creative in a sense that may depart from our usual understanding of creativity in art. In this example, the *molimo* trumpet is brought out only on life-threatening occasions. To sing to the forest awakens the forest so that it will maintain its responsibility to its children, the Pygmies. The *molimo* is an aesthetic and religious event which is creative in a primary sense. It creates life. The *molimo* is not a reflection upon the nature of life and reality, nor is it a symbolic statement about what life should be like to be used as a goal or idea. In either of these senses it would be creative in a secondary or simply artistic sense. For the Pygmy, as for many nonliterate people, many aesthetic acts are at once religious acts and must be so because life utterly depends upon them.

It follows that we may never appreciate some aspects of the art of nonliterate cultures without also appreciating the contexts in which art is produced, especially when our understanding of art is so heavily focused upon objects of art. These objects may be only the tools or the leftovers of a meaningful and creative event. If we do not know the event or its significance, we can scarcely understand the by-products we consider, perhaps in error from the

---

[3] *Ibid.,* p. 83.

point of view of their makers, as art objects. The Pygmy peoples are not typical of nonliterate cultures, and we need not hope to find their religious and aesthetic values universally held among these many diverse cultures. What we hope to achieve through the introduction of these ideas is a stance of sensitivity from which to approach more meaningfully the arts and religions of these cultures. Let us turn now to other examples.

DESTRUCTIBLE AND DISPOSABLE
ART OBJECTS

We commonly find observers of nonliterate peoples who are confounded by attitudes of apparent disregard for objects of art and religion. For example, in the late nineteenth century a man named Washington Matthews became acquainted with ritual sandpainting practiced by the Navajo in the American Southwest. He observed elaborate pictures constructed by sprinkling finely ground sands of various colors upon the floor of ceremonial houses. Deeply impressed with the beauty and complexity of these paintings, he was taken aback when he saw them being destroyed within a short time of their completion. He declared these pictures to be the most transient in the history of human art. But when we look at the art of Navajo sandpainting in its religious context, we find that this destruction of a sacred art object is no sacrilege nor violation of aesthetic values; quite the contrary. Sandpainting is performed in ceremonials to cure ailing persons by identifying them with the cosmic designs depicted in the paintings. The cosmic powers represented as humanlike beings are present in the sandpainting when properly prepared. The ailing person sits on the middle of the sandpainting and is physically identified with each element in it. Pinches of sand are placed on the body parts of the ailing person which were taken from the corresponding body parts of all the figures in the painting. It is through the use, and therefore also the destruction, of this object that a person is given life and health. The act, not the object, bears both the religious and aesthetic values. Navajos believe that sandpaintings must be destroyed by sundown on the day they are made, and no visual record is kept.

Many scholars have been confounded by the common incidence in prehistoric rock art wherein one scene is etched or painted directly over another. We may think of examples such as those at Camonica Valley in the Italian Alps. If we insist that the object produced by the graphic work must bear the aesthetic values, we can only conclude from what we observe that these values are confused. Yet, if we were to know the context, be it ceremonial or otherwise, we might find that the objects served the meaning of these events. This perspective would hold that these pictures are just the leftovers from some cultural event in the context of which they were meaningful. This view has not yet been taken by students of these works of art.

We can see another example in the *kiva* wall painting of the Pueblo peoples in North America. From prehistoric times murals have been painted on the walls of ceremonial chambers to present an environment or setting appropriate to ceremonial occasions. As the seasons pass and the ceremonial cycle advances, the old murals are whitewashed and new ones painted. We might be shocked by this act, especially seeing the beauty of the murals, but we must see that from the Pueblo perspective the art objects must serve the occasion and are of little significance apart from it.

African masks are commonly collected by Westerners as art objects, but this is not necessarily the view of Africans. To the people of Cameroun in Central Africa, for example, masks come to life only when worn by properly attired dancers performing to music. Apart from this context, the masks are little more than dead wood.

It seems that our perspective on art is inadequate to support an understanding of these objects from the perspective of the cultures which produce them. It forces us to look in the wrong places for art. It prevents us from recognizing that art and religion are inseparable from the human endeavor to participate in and maintain creative activities. On this point I am reminded of the essay written by Imamu Amiri Baraka (formerly LeRoi Jones) entitled "Hunting is Not Those Heads on the Wall." He criticizes the history of Western art for what he considers a worship of art objects. He feels that the price paid for this emphasis is the failure to appreciate the creative processes of art. In his view, art objects are what is left over from the art process, and they have no more to do with art than hunting trophies have to do with the hunt. Our examples show a kinship to this idea, but they differ in that at least certain art processes in nonliterate cultures cannot be separated from religious processes. We must appreciate the point of view found in nonliterate cultures that reverence for the artistic products or the tools of religion can become a kind of tyranny which stifles the full expression of ideas and the proper performance of religious acts. This is no small point since these acts are creative in a primary sense; they literally make life possible. There is an undeniable honesty and sensibility in this view.

SOUND IN ART AND RELIGION

The symbolic medium most central to and most common among the many diverse nonliterate cultures is sound, especially as it is formed in song, prayer, story, and poetry. In other words, sound, as communicated via the human voice, is a predominant and distinctive feature of nonliterate cultures. As we saw in the Pygmy ritual, there is a close association between acts of speech and life itself. We often find that nonliterate peoples hold speech to be more highly sacred than they do objects of any kind. This belief suggests to us that the aesthetic and religious significance of sound in nonliterate cultures should be considered more closely. Eskimo culture provides illuminating examples.

In Eskimo language, the word meaning "to breathe" also means "to make poetry," and it is rooted in the word denoting the eternal life force. It is no surprise that priest and poet are one in Eskimo culture. Orpingalik, Netsilik Eskimo poet and shaman, was articulate about these matters in conversations he had with Knud Rasmussen, who led a major expedition among the Eskimo in the 1920s.

It became clear to Rasmussen that Orpingalik linked his power as hunter and shaman closely to his songs. As shaman, Orpingalik could communicate with spirits while in a trance, and he had his own guardian spirits whose strengths and abilities he could call upon by the use of their spirit songs. His source of strength and power was in his song and poetry. Through them he could gain the power to hunt successfully, to travel safely, to cure, and even to bring harm to his enemies. His poetry was his possession and others could not use it. Orpingalik went so far as to identify his very being with his songs. He said, "All my being is song and I sing as I draw breath."[4]

We may see here reflections of the Pygmies' drainpipe *molimo*. For the Eskimo, songs are not things to be sung simply for amusement or even for their beauty. They are life. They are breath.

For the Pygmy and the Eskimo, sound and the power of speech are identified with life. Speech is impossible without breath. The spoken word emerges from the breast, from the region of the heart and lungs, and is itself evidence of vitality, of life. The act of speech has a life of its own. As words or sounds are born from the mouth or musical instrument, they live and move, but their life is short and leaves no traces.

The vitality and dynamics, even the transient quality, of sound may affect the aesthetic values of plastic art. A look at Eskimo carving can demonstrate this factor.

Contemporary stone carvings of the Eskimo are well known, but this is a quite recent development arising to meet the economic needs of Eskimo peoples. I certainly do not wish to suggest anything negative about these very beautiful works of art, but simply to point out that they arise out of a situation heavily influenced by Eskimo contact with Western civilization and consequently bear many ideas related to Western art history. Still they stand in continuity with a long history of carving, which has been an Eskimo tradition for many centuries. It is upon the roots of the carving tradition that we must focus in order to most appreciate that which is indigenous to the Eskimo.

Edmund Carpenter, in his book, *Eskimo Realities,* has pointed out that Eskimo carvers use their knives like Eskimo poets use words. For the Eskimo the use of language is the way in which they reveal the forms that are in nature, but whose significance is otherwise hidden from them. Through language things

⁴ Knud Rasmussen, *Report of the Fifth Thule Expedition, 1921–1924,* Vol. 8, Nos. 1 & 2, *The Netsilik Eskimos—Social Life and Spiritual Cultures* (Copenhagen: Gyldendalske Boghandel, 1931), pp. 16, 321.

take form; nature is revealed to be meaningful. So it is with Eskimo carvers. Taking a piece of ivory in their hands, they contemplate it, and speak to it, in order to perceive the form that it contains. They do not approach the material as raw or neutral with an intent to dominate it and make it subservient to their ideas. Rather, through their craftsmanship they permit the material to reveal its underlying or inner form. The carvers and their knives are only instruments in this process. This belief would make it difficult for an Eskimo to accept art commissions, for the material, not the patron, determines what will be carved. Art is a process in which the carver enters into a relationship with nature and perceives that process as life. Eskimo art, too, is not composed of things made but of relationships experienced, relationships critical to life. Art is dynamic, not static. It is process, not product.

Consequently, it is not surprising that the object carved is a thing to be held in the hand, not to be viewed on a shelf or in a glass case. No single visual perspective is dictated in the process, and often a range of interrelationships within a carving are revealed from various perspectives as the object is turned in the hand. The complexity of these relationships reflects essential aspects of Eskimo life.

Carpenter reports an interesting anecdote. A collector of traditional Eskimo art was faced with the difficulty of displaying his collection. Since the objects, carved to be held, often do not have flat bottoms, they tended to roll about when placed on the collector's shelf. The collector remedied the problem by filing flat bottoms. Ironically this destroyed something central to the aesthetic principles dynamically working even in the carved pieces themselves.

FIGURE 3.1. Wolf and man (Eskimo carving). (Courtesy of the Royal Ontario Museum, Toronto, Canada.)

In considering Eskimo art, Carpenter concluded that:

> The concept "art" is alien to the Eskimo, but the thing itself, the act of art, is certainly there, carefully implemented as a dimension of culture. It is not, however, always easy to recognize. The Eskimo don't put art into their environment: they treat the environment itself as art form.
>
> Such art is invisible: it belongs to that all-pervasive environment that eludes perception. It serves as a means of merging the individual and his environment, not as a means of training his perception upon that environment.[5]

ART IS A PROCESS

Through these examples we can see more and more clearly that what we should consider as art is not limited to expressive functions; it quite often embraces relations of a life-giving character. Art is never static and cannot be confined to things. We might want to adopt the term *arting*, coined by Baraka in his previously mentioned article, to help us remember that the art of nonliterate peoples is often a process of creating and maintaining life-giving relationships.

The appropriateness of the term *arting* is never more obvious than in the case of African art that is usually "danced." In recent decades the art of nonliterate peoples has received widespread attention in the Western art world, where it is always referred to as primitive art. African art has been in the limelight cast by admiring remarks by Western artists of such stature as Picasso and Matisse. Still, the overwhelming proportion of interest in this art has been confined to the art objects and almost invariably from a perspective completely ignorant of the cultures and cultural events in which these objects have meaning and life. Given the probability of misunderstanding, of misuse, and of error that such an approach brings to the art of nonliterate peoples, we may begin to appreciate another dimension of the wisdom in their common practice of discarding, destroying, or defacing the leftovers from arting. In one sense, the objects are no more art than are the sculptor's mallet and chisel or the painter's palette and brushes. Let us look at an example.

A revolution of sorts was begun in the understanding of African art when Robert Thompson published *African Art in Motion*. His insight into the nature of African art is apparent in the title and in Thompson's opening words:

> The Tiv people of Nigeria use a basic verb which means "to dance." The word, *vine,* unites the dance with further worlds of artistic happening. . . . This broad conception of the dance is widely shared in subsaharan Africa, *viz.* that dance is not restricted to the moving human body, but can combine in certain contexts

---

[5] Edmund Carpenter, *Eskimo Realities* (New York: Holt, Rinehart & Winston, 1973), pp. 202–3.

with things and objects, granting them autonomy in art, intensifying the aliveness an image must embody to function as a work of art.[6]

Thus, Thompson introduces us to a history of what he calls *danced art,* turning our attention from the fascination of objects as displayed in our museum cases and galleries to the significance of a whole cultural complex in which movement and sculpture are blended in dance with a primary creative effect.

An impressive example of African sculpture which may illustrate this point is the Epa mask of the Yoruba of Nigeria. At the base of the mask is a Janus helmet (a helmet on which two faces are carved, one looking forward, the other backward) upon which is a representation of realistic figures sometimes supported by a tray. The masks are commonly three to four feet high and may weigh more than fifty pounds. To dance the masks requires someone of considerable physical strength, and this in itself is closely associated with the religious significance of the mask. As Thompson's findings show, Africans hold youthfulness and strength in such esteem that they have religious significance. It is appropriate that only a strong man can support the Epa mask, for the occasion of the dance is the transformation of young men into adults. The display of

FIGURE 3.2. Yoruba Epa mask performance (Africa). (Photo by Marsha Vander Heyden. Used by permission.)

_____

[6] Robert F. Thompson, *African Art in Motion: Icon and Art* (Los Angeles: University of California Press, 1974), p. xii.

strength and youthfulness expressed in their masked dance is evidence of their capability to lead and protect their people. On these occasions dance and sculpture are joined through musical drama, not to artfully comment upon the nature of life, but rather to enact that art which is itself life.[7]

CONCLUSION

Since much of the religious belief and thought of nonliterate peoples are borne in physical objects and in the processes which produce these objects, several factors have been shown to be especially important if we are to understand and appreciate the religious significance of those objects of nonliterate cultures we usually identify by the term *art*. As we have shown, it does not always make sense to divide these art objects into religious and secular categories. The most utilitarian of objects, like a house or a bowl, may have high religious significance. Further, objects we find aesthetically attractive, like Navajo sandpaintings and African masks, may have, in isolation, little religious significance. They may even be viewed negatively from a religious perspective if they are retained as objects to be displayed for their beautiful appearance. We have shown that much of the significance of artifacts is inseparable from the context of the cultural and religious processes and associated beliefs and principles from which they rise. It is very rare that even a hint of this dimension is available in our museum displays and art collections because so often the display can contain only the leavings of a religiously meaningful process.

In these several examples, we have also discerned that nonliterate peoples commonly base their ideas of beauty on those human processes and actions by which they carry out their responsibility for maintaining the cosmos, that is, for keeping order and meaning in their world. Art and religion are here inseparable. By realizing this fact we can also gain a new appreciation about the kind of creativity in which nonliterate peoples may engage. By Western standards, we commonly evaluate their art as overly repetitive and lacking innovation; we place it in functional, decorative, or craft categories. Now we should see that commonly these objects come about as a result of human actions which are creative in the primary sense, that is, in the sense of bearing cosmic responsibilities, in the sense of making life possible.

---

[7] *Ibid.*, pp. 191-98.

4

the legacy: religion and modes of sustenance

"You are what you eat" is a commonly heard expression. It is often associated with cautions against eating chemical perservatives or nonnutritive foods. It is a maxim of our time, yet in it is a truth which has been recognized throughout the history of human existence. Everywhere we find people relating in special and symbolic ways to the food that sustains them, to the sources of their food, and to the manner in which they procure their food. In the previous chapters I have been especially concerned in showing that the religions of nonliterate peoples are affairs of seeing and living in realities which are richly meaningful and complex. I have hoped to show that things which are seemingly common aspects of life are never merely what they appear to be, that even the apparently commonplace matters of shelter, food, and sex can be the means for living and expressing one's religiousness. Drainpipes, cooking pots, houses, and skull bones may all serve to reveal the richness and meaning of life. I have wanted to emphasize the importance of being able to understand these data as religious, especially in the study of nonliterate peoples, where we have no written histories, creeds, or dogmas upon which to base our understanding of their religions.

In this chapter I want to extend this point further by considering the legacy which contemporary nonliterate peoples and certainly all of humanity have received from the long history of human existence. The legacy to which I refer is the correspondence of certain types of religious beliefs and expressions to the most basic modes of sustenance in the history of human existence—hunting and agriculture.

Although in the long run there may be nothing particularly revealing in describing types of religion on the basis of modes of sustenance, it has certainly been a compelling means of classification because of the nature of our data about the peoples of the prehistoric past. Our knowledge of the religions of these peoples is limited to our ability to read and interpret archaeological artifacts. It has been only during the last century that most of the data from human prehistory have come to light. Of course, most of the effort to interpret these data has been devoted to the construction of a chronology of human existence divided into periods and eras. It is the nature of artifactual data that they should speak much more clearly to us about modes of sustenance and levels of the development of material culture than about religious belief and action. After all, archaeologists find tools, bones, and pots, not songs, prayers, and stories. These religious matters survive only as they are very dimly reflected in the more permanent objects of culture which have survived. Consequently, scholars have accounted for the history of human growth and development during the greatest portion of the period of human existence in terms of material culture and the modes of sustenance evidenced in the material objects of culture. Scholars have scarcely been free to interpret the religions of prehistory in any terms other than those closely linked with modes of sustenance.

In our Western way of interpreting and describing the significance of human cultures in terms of their relationship to the past, the broad outline of a picture emerges from the prehistoric period. Since the appearance of humanity, some one to two million years ago, human beings sustained themselves primarily by hunting and gathering until the invention of agriculture a modest ten thousand years ago. The distinct histories of the great religions of the world have occurred within the period of the last five thousand years. The shared legacy from the immense era of human existence before that time has been distinguished principally in the terms of sustenance—hunting and agriculture.

From vast bodies of diverse data, there has emerged the notion that there are certain general affinities between religious ideologies and forms of symbolic expression and these modes of sustenance. These have been accepted as basic categories by which we may interpret certain aspects of the history of religions. Since nonliterate peoples have tended throughout the histories of their cultures to be dependent principally upon these basic modes of sustenance, and since the religious data of nonliterate peoples of all times are to a degree opaque because of the fact of nonliteracy, these interpretive categories are especially significant to our present concern.

We may begin the outline of these categories by a presentation of some examples from early hunting peoples.

THE EARLY HUNTERS

Early in this century archaeologists began to make numerous finds which shed a little light on the religions of early hunters. Some of these were bear skulls and bones dating from the early Paleolithic era, more than half a million years ago.

The correlation of human existence with these bones is remarkable evidence of the human habitation in the Swiss Alps and the surrounding area at this early time. But more notable is that the evidence related to these bear bones, especially the skulls, suggests human intentions of a religious character. In one cave at some eight thousand feet of elevation near Drachenloch, Switzerland, seven well-preserved bear skulls were found in a stone chest, all facing the cave entrance. Other skulls were similarly oriented in nitches along the wall. Some skulls had the long bones of other bears inserted through the arches of their cheekbones. Similar evidence was found in other caves.

Evidence dating much later, from the upper Paleolithic era and into the last ice age, has been found which suggests the ritual treatment of bears. Skulls show indications that the canine and incisor teeth had been filed off shortly before the bears had died. There are numerous engravings on cave walls depicting bears which appear to be pierced with arrows and are bleeding profusely.

In A. I. Hallowell's major study of bear ceremonialism made early in this century, he demonstrated that there are general similarities to this treatment of bear bones among recent circumpolar hunting peoples. There are striking similarities in the treatment of bear skulls and bones among many northern hunting peoples. The similarity of an apparently ritual treatment of bear bones which is datable over a very long period of time has suggested to many scholars that bear ceremonialism has been an aspect of the religions of a wide range of hunting peoples from the early Paleolithic era. Given these facts, a number of interpretations of the early religious practices of hunting peoples have been made. I do not feel that these are sufficiently provable to present here, but what is fairly clear, I think, is that these early hunters saw that the nature of life was, in part, bound up with their life-and-death relationship with the animals they killed and ate; they also perceived that the meaning of this relationship was deeper than the commonplace concerns of procuring food.

Another stunning example of the expression of early hunting peoples has come to light in this century. In some of the caves in France magnificent paintings datable to the last ice age have been found. Most of these paintings are of animals and are located in almost inaccessible parts of the caves, which has suggested to interpreters that the paintings must have had some special significance not solely explainable as decoration. Scholars in the early part of this century believed that early man thought that to depict a thing in pictorial form was to gain control over it. Consequently, they have interpreted these paintings as examples of a primitive ritual hunting magic. They argued that for the early hunter, to paint the animal's picture was to gain magical control over it. The semantic opacity and great antiquity of this evidence make explanation hypothetical at best, but we might suggest an alternative to this magic-oriented view. It would seem as likely that the very act of depiction might have mediated the necessary spiritual relationships between hunter and game. The cave paintings are often made one on top of another, and many have numerous marks, usually considered to be spears or stones, drawn over the figures. If we shift from

FIGURE 4.1. Death of a hunter (cave drawing, Lascaux).

a perspective which views only the present state of the paintings, and these as finished works of art, to one which would be concerned with the processes and actions involved in creating the markings whose remains we now have, we may suggest that it was the act of making the drawing which was instrumental to accomplishing or instigating spiritual relationships, and that the finished drawings were, in themselves, of no particular value.

Another remarkable example from the last ice age suggests one aspect of the religions of prehistoric hunting peoples. As the ice age was coming to a close, hunters followed herds of reindeer far north to the edge of the receding ice during the summer months. Coincidentally, in the Near East and in America, the invention of agriculture was taking place. The most telling finds were made at Meiendorf in northern Germany in 1935. The discoveries were made in a low

FIGURE 4.2. Rhino hunt (rock art, Nauzerus, Naukluft Mountains, Africa). (From Jalmar and Ione Rudner, *The Hunter and His Art. A Survey of Rock Art in Southern Africa.* Cape Town: Struik, 1970. Courtesy Jalmar and Ione Rudner.)

area with lakes formed by the ice melt. In one of these ancient lake beds were found several complete skeletons of reindeer with heavy stones in their thoracic cavities. The skeletons were wholly intact and were invariably two-year-old does. Further evidence indicates that they had been killed by a weapon. The growth of the antlers still attached indicates that they were killed at the beginning of the summer season. A reconstruction of how this condition might have come about suggests that these were sacrificial animals. It is imagined that at the beginning of the hunt a suitable animal was killed, and the hunters would open its chest and place stones in the cavity. Then, perhaps accompanied by certain rites, they would submerge the animal in the lake as a sacrifice of first fruits.

I do not wish to press these prehistoric examples to any detailed interpretations, for I believe that we simply do not have sufficient evidence to do so. Still, this brief presentation is sufficient to illustrate several points and to show something of the nature of the data which are available from these early cultures. The examples show us how opaque the data are in terms of the evidence they bear about the religions of these peoples. That is, the examples help us to appreciate how difficult it is to know much of anything about the religions of these early hunters. But even with this difficulty, it does not seem to stretch our data too far to suggest in very general terms that these early hunters were religious and that the beliefs, as well as the expression, of their religions were inseparable from the animals whose death gave them life. The symbols by which they came

FIGURE 4.3. Bora ritual: symbolic spearing of a kangaroo. (From Ronald M. Berndt, *Australian Aboriginal Religion,* 1974. Courtesy of E. J. Brill.)

to know and to express their beliefs about the nature of existence must have clustered around game animals and the life-and-death relationship which involved hunting, butchering, and eating. It is most important that we understand that these relatively commonplace actions must have been invested with the highest meaning for the individual and the social group in which he or she lived.

The presentation of a much fuller example of the religion of a hunting culture, the Naskapi, whose culture, hunting ways, and religious beliefs and actions were documented extensively in this century, will help to show how important and persistent is this legacy of hunting.

The Naskapi

The Labrador Peninsula in eastern Canada is the homeland of the Naskapi, a nomadic people who are sustained primarily by hunting and who live in a culture whose technology and material goods differ little from Mesolithic hunting peoples of ten to fifteen thousand years ago.[1] As their lives are dependent upon and heavily occupied with matters of animals, their view of the world and their religious beliefs are lived and expressed extensively in terms of animals. Recalling the passage of the Carrier man in Chapter 1, who said his ancestors married and lived with animals, we find the existence of this same closeness to animals among the Naskapi. From their perspective, animals were people in the primal era and had characteristics of both human beings and animals. They lived much as do the Naskapi, had the same social structure, and had the power of human speech. Once the primal era came to a close, the animal peoples lost their human appearances but retained, especially in their inner life forms, their personhood. The Naskapi can, therefore, maintain a personal relationship with the life spirits of animals, a relationship mediated through dreams, songs, drumming, and artistic activities (arting) with the aid of sorcerers and diviners.

Proper relationships with animals must be maintained because life virtually depends upon them. The life cycles of animals and human beings are interlocked and interdependent. The immortal life form (soul or spirit) of the animal is engaged in a cyclic process of bearing its animal's flesh, which is given to the hunter in response to his respect and symbolic gifts. The proper killing and use of the animal's body releases the life form and permits it to return to its home, where it can regenerate another physical form.

For the Naskapi hunting is a religious activity, a major means for living a religious life and expressing religious beliefs, but not the sum total of their religion.

Let us look now at the practices related to two animals, the caribou and the bear, in order to discuss religious aspects of widespread incidence among hunting peoples.

---

[1] Frank G. Speck, *Naskapi: The Savage Hunters of the Labrador Peninsula* (Norman: University of Oklahoma Press, 1935).

THE CARIBOU. The caribou is the most important source of food for the Naskapi, who consider them to be a race of highly intelligent animal people living much as humans do. It is believed that the caribou migrate into human territory annually in order to give their flesh to the hunters who need it so desperately for food. During the remainder of the year they live in their home under the control of a master, Caribou Man.

Stories trace the origin of the Caribou Man to a human hunter who took it upon himself to protect the animals and to make sure that hunters take no more than they need and are not wasteful with what they take. Described as a white man dressed in black, he is master of the caribou home, a place forbidden to human beings. In stories, Caribou House is envisioned as a dome-shaped mountain resembling a wigwam. It is white in color because it is covered with caribou hair, as is the surrounding area for miles. The caribou hair and antlers are piled to what would be waist deep on a human being. When the young caribou leave their home only their heads can be seen above the hair and antlers. This Caribou House is the home of thousands upon thousands of caribou.

To the Naskapi hunters, which include both men and women, the success of a hunt is primarily dependent upon their spiritual preparation, the willingness of the beasts, and the permission of the master of the animals. A successful hunt is not possible without these religious affairs being in order. Weapons are auxiliary to the hunt; they are instrumental to the complex relationship between hunter and animal. The physical relationship mediated by weapons is possible only as a result of the establishment of an intimate spiritual relationship between hunters and animals mediated by the master of animals. Hunting is not the human dominance of animals. The role of hunters begins by being sensitive to the revelations and visitations of animal spirits which give them knowlege of the animal's whereabouts and the power to lure the animals to them. These spiritual preparations often require the use of drumming, which is a means of obtaining revelation. The drum is considered a person, and when it is beaten—the customary manner is a very rapid beating of five or six beats a second—sensitive hunters can hear the messages from the spirit world which are spoken through the drum. Hunters must know how to treat animals respectfully, how to properly kill them, and how to utilize their bodies for food and essential cultural objects.

THE BEAR. The bear is an animal which is also of great importance to the Naskapi, and although it is not depended upon so much for food as the caribou, it is the subject of more elaborate ritual treatment because, according to the people, the bear has supremacy over the other animals and has physical features and intelligence similar to humans. The inner spirit of the bear is one of the great powers among all animal spirits. Bear hunting is performed in a highly ritualized manner, which begins with preparations in a sweat bath and does not conclude until the bear carcass is completely used. The hunters go to the den of the bear as spring approaches and address the bear as ''grandfather'' or ''grandmother,'' depending on its sex. They apologize for their need to kill it and thank it for giving itself to them that they might live on its flesh. There are rules about the dressing of the carcass and the distribution and preparation of each part of the bear. The entire social structure finds its order in this procedure, which includes a ceremonial feast with dancing and singing. In fact, a chart of the bear carcass on the order of a butcher's chart of a side of beef would be something of a map of the social structure. The bear plays the central role in this affair, and its skull is decorated with paint and mounted on a pole or suspended from a tree, where it serves as an important religious object for the people as they move about throughout the year.

Keeping in mind our discussions of time, space, and art, we can see that these hunters' treatment of and relationship with animals reflect their view of the world and what they understand to be the meaning of human life. They do not see their relationship with animals in the simple pragmatic terms of so many servings of meat; instead, they see the incredible complexity and profundity of the relationship among living things which permits life and gives it continuity and meaning. This relationship, this view of life, cannot be perceived in other than the most personal terms, the terms of a human being and the food which sustains him; yet it must also address life, in the most universal terms, in the terms of immortal animal spirits and the master of the animals.

This kind of relationship between humans and animals is not peculiar to the Naskapi, for it is found among hunting peoples the world over, as is the presence of various forms of the master of animals. Debate among scholars has left little clear notion of how the master of animals relates to the theologies and total religious systems of hunting peoples, but we might expect that its broad incidence does not require that it be related to the same religious ideas wherever it occurs. Indeed, a careful examination of several occurrences of the master of animals (ranging, for example, from the Caribou Man of the Naskapi to Sedna, the Mother of the Sea Animals of the Eskimo) assures us that a great range of religious ideas may be borne within this form and that each of these cultures has its own history of the development of religious ideas and forms of expression.

THE INVENTION OF AGRICULTURE

The invention of agriculture sparked one of the great revolutions in human history. There are certain types of religious beliefs and actions whose origins can be traced to this revolution. The basic relationship of the hunter to his sustenance was that of the receiver to a gift. For the cultivators, that relationship was changed in a fundamental way for they became the producers of their food. People's relationship with the world in which they lived necessarily had to undergo fundamental alterations. Instead of living at the pleasure of the game or the master of the animals, by following animals as they moved about, human communities which cultivated their food began to see the dimensions of the whole cosmos as coincident with the very places where they had settled to grow their crops. The house, the village, the fields became invested with cosmic significance; they were seen as microcosmic. Not only did the understanding of space undergo transformation, so also did the human relationship to time. Agriculture required the development of more precise temporal calculations so that meteorological conditions could be anticipated in correlation with the agricultural cycle. The expression of religious belief in terms of the relationships with the animal world, so important to the hunters, gave way to that of the relationships with vegetation, the earth, the meteorological phenomena. Doubtless the beliefs themselves underwent extensive transformations as well. Fundamental to the religious beliefs of agricultural peoples is the mystery of birth, death, and rebirth, which is constantly portrayed in the rhythms of vegetation. Common to the religious practices of agriculturalists is the periodic renewal of the world, a renewal of the cosmos brought about by the repetition of the cosmogony, the acts by which the world has been created.

Then, too, there is a shift from the emphasis on masculinity in hunting cultures to a much greater emphasis on female and maternal roles, although hunters have not been exclusively masculine. The dominant role women have played in agricultural activities is notable, but it has to do with more than a simple division of labor. The vegetation process has been associated broadly with sexuality and fertility. In this context, the feminine and maternal roles have been of major importance in portraying the religious world views of agricultural peoples.

Hunting did not simply give way to agriculture. Indeed, few agricultural peoples have not engaged in occasional hunting activities. Thus, an already complex situation is compounded manyfold as hunting and agricultural beliefs and symbols of expression merge and develop over long histories among many diverse cultures.

The agriculturally related religious ideas may be presented more clearly by an example of a contemporary agricultural people, the Dogon of Africa.

The Dogon

The Dogon live in Upper Volta in the western Sudan. Beyond the view it gives of religious beliefs and expressions associated with an agricultural people the example of the Dogon is remarkable because of the information we have about their religious thought. It has often been incorrectly assumed that nonliterate peoples do not engage extensively in intellectual thought nor in metaphysical matters. It has been supposed that intellectual development has coincided with material development. This view has been discussed and rejected by a number of scholars[2] although there is still a tendency to hold to it. The knowledge of Dogon

---

[2] See, for example, Claude Levi-Strauss, *The Savage Mind* (Chicago: The University of Chicago Press, 1966).

religious ideas is available to us largely because of an extraordinary opportunity of anthropologist Marcel Griaule. After he had been associated with the Dogon for some fifteen years he was one day unexpectedly summoned to the home of an old blind Dogon man, and in regular conversations which took place between Griaule and the old man, whose name was Ogotemmêli, the great depth, complexity, and richness of Dogon religious thought came to light.[3]

This knowledge was esoteric, and throughout the conversations Ogotemmêli carefully guarded against others overhearing him. But it became clear that a select group of elders was priviledged to this knowledge and that although it could be expressed in these philosophical discussions, it was, as we shall soon see, also expressed through the Dogon way of life. Although we have only a few records of this kind of statement from individuals in nonliterate cultures, we shouldn't think that it is peculiar to the Dogon; rather we should realize that ethnographers have often not known to seek it, and perhaps also that it requires much more time than they usually have to establish the relationship that would make the revelation of this kind of information possible. Let us consider now some of the ideas told by Ogotemmêli, which reveal the Dogon beliefs about cultivation.

The Dogon prepare and cultivate fields in the area surrounding their mountain villages. Cultivation, of course, is one of the most obvious ways in which to mark out the landscape, to proclaim the meaningfulness of space. We can begin here:

"The land," said Ogotemmêli, "is cultivated in squares, eight cubits a side, surrounded by embankments of earth."

The area of each plot, he explained, is that of the flat roof of the celestial granary; and the plot is orientated so that each side faces a cardinal point of the compass.

"The old method of cultivation," he went on, "is like weaving; one begins on the north side, moving from east to west and then back from west to east. On each line eight feet are planted and the square has eight lines recalling the eight ancestors and the eight seeds."

And then Ogotemmêli continued this to tell that weaving is a form of speech, which is imparted to the fabric by the to-and-fro movement of the shuttle on the warp; and in the same way the to-and-fro movement of the peasant on his plot imparts the Word of the ancestors, that is to say, moisture, to the ground on which he works, and thus rids the earth of impurity and extends the area of cultivation round inhabited places.

But, if cultivation is a form of weaving, it is equally true to say that weaving is a form of cultivation.[4]

---

[3] Marcel Griaule, *Conversations with Ogotemmêli: An Introduction to Dogon Religious Ideas* (London: Oxford University Press, 1965).

[4] *Ibid.*, pp. 76–77.

This is a remarkably compact statement of the Dogon cosmicization of the seemingly commonplace acts of cultivation. We need to discuss Ogotemmêli's statements to appreciate them more fully. To begin we may note the associations he made. He associates the field with a celestial granary, a structure we will need to learn more about, but it is clearly a primal structure. The plot of ground is oriented to correspond with the cosmic directions. Its dimensions of eight cubits on a side and the eight feet and eight lines identify it with the eight ancestors, whom we will discuss, and their eight seeds. He identifies the act of cultivation with the act of weaving, and then he identifies weaving with speech. Cultivation imparts to the ground the word of the ancestor, which is identified with moisture. Beyond that the act of cultivation overcomes impurity.

It becomes clear from the extent of just these associations and identifications that in cultivation the Dogon perform acts based upon the primal models of their ancestors and that in these acts, which are equivalent to speaking the sacred words of the ancestors, the world is created and impurity is dispelled.

We cannot know Ogotemmêli's statements about cultivation in their greatest depth, but we may still consider several of the ideas his remarks convey.

Of great importance is Ogotemmêli's account of the creation. He described the sacred intercourse between Amma, the one and all-powerful god, and his wife, who is associated with the earth. In this intercourse, water, which is the divine seed, entered the womb of the earth, fertilizing it, and from this act were born two spirit beings, called Nummo. Ogotemmêli spoke of them as being perfect and complete. He identified them with water and with speech. They had eight members (arms and legs), which symbolize their perfection since the number eight symbolizes completeness. Because of these primordial events the number eight, breath, and water form a symbolic complex associated with creativity. Since speech is an act of the mouth which is received by the ear, the mouth and ear become identified with sexual organs.

In their first generative acts, the Nummo, these spirit beings, spoke to themselves, and their words (water) entered their own wombs; one produced four males who were also female and the other produced four females who were also male. These became the first humans and the eight ancestors of the Dogon. Ancestral lines are traced from these eight, as are the Dogon crops, for Amma gave a different kind of seed to each ancestor. As each ancestor engaged in the sexual acts which led to his/her offspring, the perfect knowledge of words was gained, and according to Ogotemmêli, it is the mastery of words, of language, which gives the world its unity and perfection.

We can see how the primacy of speech is inseparable from every domain of creation as it is established through the words of each of the eight ancestors. Weaving, for example, was revealed by the seventh ancestor. This ancestral spirit spat out eighty threads of cotton, and these took shape as warp spanning the upper and lower teeth. Then by opening and shutting his/her jaws the spirit caused the threads to cross, and the web of the weaving took shape. Ogotemmêli said that the spirit was speaking while the work proceeded so that the weaving embodied his/her sacred words. His/her words were woven into the threads and became one with the cloth. Consequently, the Dogon call cloth *soy,* which means "it is the spoken word," and it also means "seven" for it was the seventh ancestor who revealed weaving. Ogotemmêli explained that in this word human beings came to know more of the nature of life and of their world.

Amma proceeded to give shape and distinction to the physical world which was described by Ogotemmêli in symbolic form as the "Granary of the Master of Pure Earth," that is, as the celestial granary. Dogon granaries are modeled after this cosmic structure. The symbolism is very complex. Greatly simplified, it can be described as a building of two stories with four rooms below and four above. It has exterior stairways in each of the four cardinal directions. Each step on these stairways is associated with a species of plant, animal, bird, or fish; each step is a symbol of a species. Each of the compartments in the granary is associated with one of the eight seeds, but they are not simply for storage of grain; they also represent the eight organs of the spirit of water and also the eight organs of human beings. The outer walls of the granary contain the inner organs, and the inner partitions represent the skeleton. The uprights in the four corners represent the arms and legs. Ogotemmêli summarized the structure by likening it to a woman, "lying on her back (representing the sun) with her arms and legs raised and supporting the roof (representing the sky). The two legs were on the north side, and the door at the sixth step marked the sexual parts."[5]

The granary is the representation of the shape and functioning of the world and of human life. All that is significant in the universe has its place in this granary structure, which is none other than the female human form. Drawing parallels between cosmic form and human life, Ogotemmêli told Griaule, "What is eaten is the sunlight. What is excreted is the dark night. The breath of life is the clouds, and the blood is the rain that falls on the world."[6]

This is but a glimpse of a system of religious ideas and symbols which is extremely complex, but perhaps it is sufficient to illustrate religious ideas and forms of expression broadly associated with agricultural peoples. The Dogon invest the commonplace aspects of their subsistence activities with cosmic meanings. They speak of the order of their world, the nature of life, and the creation and destiny of the world in terms of cultivation, granaries, weaving, and human digestive and sexual functions. For Ogotemmêli and his partners in esoteric knowledge, the physical world is transparent, and every building, garden plot, and human action is seen in terms of its metaphysics. Throughout their symbols and ideology, seeds are identified with and represent the earth, which is primal and feminine. The all-powerful god, Amma, who is primal and mascu-

5 *Ibid.,* p. 39.
6 *Ibid.,* p. 40.

line is associated with the sky or the heavenly domain above the earth. It was the union of Amma with his wife, who is associated with the earth, which gave birth to the creators of the ancestors. This union is replicated in the human act of cultivation. For the ordinary Dogon, the meaning of life is found in the living of it according to the way of the ancestors.

The Dogon share with many agricultural peoples the tendency to cosmicize the landscape in their immediate area of residence and especially the architecture of their houses and granaries. They view their sustenance activities as manifesting the grandest of cosmic processes, the fertilization achieved in the holy marriage of the divinities of sky and earth.

CONCLUSION

In our examples, it is notable that for the hunters the intimacy of their relationship with animals is reflected in the primacy of speech as opposed to weapons, and for the agriculturalists the processes of fertilization essential to the production of food crops is an affair of words. The understanding of the creative power of language is widespread among nonliterate peoples, and as we have seen, its power is demonstrated in the acts which are closest to the necessities of life, the modes of sustenance. The hunters speak with the animals in their spiritual or life forms. They associate speech with breath and with the life-giving and eternal spirit of the animals.

For agriculturalists, speech is associated with semen, with rain, and with the moisture of fertilization. As Ogotemmêli so eloquently put it, ''The life-force which is the bearer of the Word, which *is* the Word, leaves the mouth in the form of breath, or water vapour, which is water and is Word.''[7]

The religious legacy of archaic hunters and agriculturalists runs very deep and is strong. It persists in clearly recognizable ways among contemporary nonliterate peoples who have continued to sustain themselves according to these modes. The legacy is not absent even from the great world religions, but it may be less easy to identify.

Although the importance of the legacies of the archaic hunters and agriculturalists is undeniable, there are, nonetheless, two notes of caution which need to be sounded. First, although we have tended to describe these legacies in more or less unified terms, we are only presenting the most surface level of the forms that the religious beliefs and expressions have taken. It is quite clear that within these general forms, a wide and diverse range of beliefs may be expressed. Consequently, we cannot assume too much about the religious beliefs of a people simply by identifying their mode of sustenance. Second, as we come to

---

[7] *Ibid.*, p. 138.

know more and more about the history of religions, we may develop cetegories with which to describe the religions of archaic peoples in terms other than those of sustenance. This development will enhance our understanding of these legacies. It remains to be shown that sustenance is the best, or even a necessary, way to describe types of religion.

Karikari Poti of Asumegya

When I am on the way, do not let me meet
    Gye-me-di, the terror.
It is Karikari Poti, Gye-me-di, the terror
That spells death to those who meet him.

Pampam Yiadɔm Boakye Akum-ntɛm.
Grandchild of Karikari Poti hails from
    Asymegya Santemanso
      Where the leopard roars and comes to town
        for its prey.

O, mother,
What of your children and I.
O, mother,
Your children and I will feed on the spider,
The mouse is too big a game.[1]

It is in printed form that we most often meet the oral traditions of nonliterate peoples. Ethnographers and folklorists have filled the shelves of our libraries with

---

[1] J. H. Nketia, *Funeral Dirges of the Akan People* (New York: Negro Universities Press, 1955), pp. 57–58. The description here of these oral traditions is based on material presented in this book.

hundreds of collections. In these collections we find dozens of examples organized under headings like praise poems, riddles, aphorisms, tales, legends, myths, and we are more likely to be confused than moved by them. If we said that they often appear to be crude and of little artistic or religious significance we would be agreeing with the opinions of many. Even if we hold for them a greater sympathy, still we probably feel that these texts are surrounded by a veil of mystery which clouds our understanding.

The very nature of this sort of response must signal us to ask a few more questions before we close the book and consign these peoples to the ranks of "primitive." Most immediately striking is the form in which these *oral traditions* are available to us. Neither the aspect of tradition nor orality has survived. We read them; we neither hear nor observe them told again and again. Usually we read them in the context of only the white paper on which they are printed, bound perhaps in a book on whose cover appears the name of the people from whom they were collected and occasionally, but not always, containing some comments about geography and cultural patterns in a preface or an introductory chapter. It is quite rare that we know even the name of the raconteur(s). Since most are collected during special interviews, we often don't know the occasion on which they are usually performed in their cultures nor what other events accompany them. It is rare to find any comment by the people about the role and significance of the texts we read.

Separated from both their orality and tradition, the texts offer limited possibilities for being appreciated as oral traditions. Commonly, scholars ignore the fact that these are oral traditions and consider them as written poetry and literature, using literary critical techniques for analysis and interpretation. Some scholars have approached the universal aspects of these traditions by identifying psychological themes and archetypes. Others make use of them for a scholarly interest in determining the diffusion of culture and folklore. Although all these concerns bear a certain useful fruit, we must not forget our first sense of disappointment and confusion. We must see that because the very defining characteristics of these forms, their orality and their service to the traditions of a people, are not available to us, the results of these studies remain far short of acceptable.

Yet we need not despair, for there are occasions when we can come much closer to appreciating oral expressions, and we will discuss a number of examples in this chapter. We will use these examples to focus our discussion on aspects of oral traditions that will help us to appreciate their richness as cultural forms, as well as to introduce some fundamental ways to interpret and understand them. We will consider the importance of seeing oral traditions in the context of both their performance and their particular history. How they respond to change, address existential needs, and yet maintain tradition are all part of this history. We will consider the language (terminology) in which scholars have discussed oral traditions as well as indigenous classifications. We will consider the fundamental religious importance of types of oral traditions that have commonly been ignored by scholars of religion because they appear to be light and entertaining. This discussion will provide an introduction to the nature and scope of oral traditions; we will show that these speech acts are inseparable from the religious traditions of nonliterate peoples.

AKAN FUNERAL DIRGES AND THE IMPORTANCE OF THE PERFORMANCE CONTEXT

The text which opens this chapter is taken from a very important book, *Funeral Dirges of the Akan,* by an African author, J. H. Nketia. This dirge, confronted out of its proper context, cannot convey much meaning, and we will show how much of the significance of the text is dependent upon its performance as a religious act and on the beliefs of the people who perform and witness this oral form. Of course, no amount of description can replace an actual performance, but our imaginations may help reduce the difference.

Let us imagine ourselves in an Akan town on the Gold Coast of West Africa. The occasion is that of the death of an old woman, mother to many. As she draws her last breath, the old woman is given a little water so that she may be properly prepared for her journey to the next world. It is the sacred duty of her children to give her this water. Messengers are sent to inform relatives in the town and in nearby villages of the death. The family washes and prepares her body. The doors of the house remain closed, indicating the privacy of this act, and it is done calmly and without mourning. The mourners begin to arrive at the house, and when the old woman's body is ready for viewing, the doors of the house are flung open, permitting the mourners to enter and signaling the start of public mourning.

As we enter with the mourners we see the relatives, young and old, sobbing and wailing as they approach the old woman's body. They call her "mother" and "grandmother" and express their grief to her. The men come also, but they do not wail; that is the expression of women. More and more relatives arrive, expressing their grief and taking places on stools and on the floor around the body. Women, usually middle aged and older, begin in pulsating and wailing voices to sing the funeral dirges. Surrounded on every side by the many members of their lineage they pace back and forth in front of the old woman's body. From time to time they pause at the corpse or in front of the old woman's closest relatives to sing their dirges. Bodies and heads gently and gracefully rocking, they turn to one side and the other as they sing. Their hands, folded on their breasts or supported on their heads, convey their anguish, as does the cincture of cloth tied around their upper bodies. Though they do not dance, their facial expressions and all their body movements express their anguish.

As the mourning continues, the singing of dirges becomes a constant presence, with several being sung at once. Amidst the cacophony of weeping and wailing we hear a sobbing woman sing in a wailing voice

Karikari Poti of Asumegya

When I am on the way, do not let me meet
Gye-me-di, the terror
It is Karikari Poti, Gye-me-di, the terror
That spells death to those who meet him. . . .

We can feel the weight of this terror that acknowledges the death in our presence. It is in the body and voice of the singer as well as in her words. Sung well, a dirge will move even the men to tears.

Bands of musicians arrive to sing laments during this period of public mourning, but the singing of dirges continues. When the coffin is brought in and the old woman's body is placed in it for burial, the mourning reaches its emotional peak. There is much wailing and many dirges are intensely sung. In recent times burial often takes place on the day of the death or the day following, but in the past the body would not be buried for several days. Only a few mourners accompany the coffin to burial, and they may wail and sing dirges.

After burial the postfuneral mourning begins and continues for several days. During this time drumming, singing, and dancing gradually displace the wailing and singing of dirges, yet these may intermittently erupt with intensity. As the mourners fast during the period of mourning, they gradually exhaust themselves.

The singing of the dirge is central to Akan funeral customs, and all women are expected to participate. Dirges are not sung outside the occasion of a funeral or the days of mourning which remember dead members of various households. Nketia found it difficult to record dirges, for women explained that they could not utter the words without shedding tears or fasting. The dirge provides an appropriate outlet for grief and its singing helps establish the prevailing mood of anguish and sorrow that befits the occasion of death. Whereas the elements of the performance are essential, the content and message of the dirge are also significant and reflect the religious world view of the Akan.

According to Nketia's analysis of the form of dirges, we can recognize that the one previously quoted is centered around the themes of the ancestor, the deceased, and the place of domicile. It opens by naming an ancestor and the place with which the ancestor is associated. This is followed by the principal subject of the dirge, a message to the ancestor. The deceased is then named, followed by a closing passage serving to connect the deceased with the ancestor. The dirge may conclude here or it may be extended, as is the one quoted. In that case the mourner elects to address the dead with praise or with a message or to reflect upon her own plight.

We may better appreciate the formal structure of the dirge if we know something of the Akan beliefs about death, afterlife, and the role of ancestors. Death is regarded as the occasion when a deceased person begins a journey to the spirit world, which is an underworld where he must settle his account with his ancestors who have gone before him. Although the journey is difficult and full of dangers, this is still the desired destiny because the wicked will not be accepted in this spirit world and their disembodied spirits will have no place. Ancestors play a role as spiritual beings in the governance of the world, and it is essential that the lineage of ancestors be remembered. The occasion of death is one on which the remembrance and communication with the ancestors is particularly appropriate and immanently possible, for upon death the dead connect the world of the living to the world of the ancestral spirits in the funeral rite of passage. Not only may the ancestors be remembered and honored, but also the one newly dead who is to become an ancestor must be associated with them.[2] This function gives structure to the dirge we have quoted. Let us look at it one more time to put all these elements together.

The dirge opens with the name, Karikari Poti, who is an ancestor of the deceased and of the mourners, and this ancestor is associated with the place named Asumegya. The subject of the dirge which follows is a message to the ancestor asking that the dirge singer not meet with the terror which is death, named *Gye-me-di*. It means ''believe me'' and consequently is a strong name given a person who is to be taken seriously.

Next the deceased is named, Pampam Yiadɔm Boakye Akum-ntɛm, and is identified as kin to the ancestor; she is placed with the ancestor at Asymegya Santemanso, a forest area associated in the olden days with being greatly menaced by leopards, as the dirge recalls. To this point the dirge serves to remember an ancestor of the lineage, to send him a message, and to link the deceased with the ancestor. But the singer extends the dirge with her personal message to the deceased. It has to do with her own plight and that of the other living relatives of the old woman.

> *O, mother,*
> *What of your children and I.*

This thought follows a theme common to these extensions. It portrays the feelings of the living and honors the dead by indicating that the living will fare worse without them, that they will suffer privations. The deceased is thus represented as one who has made important contributions to the life of the group. This theme is reiterated in the figurative language which ends the dirge.

> *O, mother,*
> *Your children and I will feed on the spider,*
> *The mouse is too big a game.*

---

[2] Numerous African stories about death can be found in Hans Abrahamsson, *The Origin of Death: Studies In African Mythology* (New York: Arno Press, 1977).

For this Akan funeral dirge, as for this aspect of Akan oral traditions, the veil of mystery we may have felt has parted a little and we can see the far-reaching artistic and religious significance borne in the performance of the dirge. The mystery that remains no longer blocks our view but is at the heart of what we see. The mystery is the wonder that something so rich, so appropriate, so complex, yet so simple, should exist at all. Indeed, for me, this is the first and final attraction to oral traditions and other forms of symbolic expression, that they exist at all. Surely the more we come to grasp the profundity of oral traditions, the more we will find endless amazement at this testimony to the capacity and ingenuity of the human potential for expression.

But we have laid aside points which need to be further considered. Recalling our discussion of art and art processes in nonliterate cultures, we can see that there is continuity here with the area of oral traditions. Akan women cannot simply recite a dirge on command or request; it must be *performed*. Only when we see the text as an oral performance in the appropriate cultural and religious contexts can we begin to appreciate it from the perspective of the Akan people. Any attempt to appreciate oral traditions on the basis of a written text isolated from its culture is something akin to trying to appreciate a ballet by reading the musical score of the violin in the orchestra. If we know the ballet, we might well see that the violin carries many of the major themes, but what an enormous loss to our eyes, ears, and hearts if this is all we are ever permitted to see.

We must also mention again the notion of creativity, in the sense of innovation and uniqueness, concerning this Akan example. According to Nketia's analysis the dirge can be any of several types, but the structure of each type is always predictable and the formal elements are defined by the themes which they state. Even the language of these themes is fairly closely prescribed by convention, and in the extension passages, where greatest self-expression is permitted, there still are common phrasings of the kinds of themes that are appropriate. Nevertheless, as Nketia has shown, even with these restrictions the dirge is a means of expression, the success and appropriateness of which are tied to the very structure that defines and confines it. Holding to the structure of the dirge, the singer has the means by which to respond to the occasion of death in a manner appropriate to her feelings and her responsibilities as a relative. On the occasion of the performance of the dirge, it is obvious that these are not wooden, memorized passages recited only because tradition calls for them. They permit expression of grief appropriate within a religious view of the world.

THE STORY OF HAINUWELE: THE HISTORY AND APPLICATION OF ORAL TRADITIONS

Folklorists have commonly warned us, and rightly so, that studying a culture on the basis of the tale types and the motifs of its lore is prone to problems. They point out that very diverse cultures commonly hold stories which are at one level virtually the same. The folklorist is interested in universal elements in the tales, and also in the history of the movement or diffusion of tale types from area to area and culture to culture. But for all this, it seems to me that a bit too much emphasis has been given to the eternal sameness of these oral expressions. The assumption implies that the tale is no more than its types and motifs and that these have specific places and times of origin. To this concern for the history of the diffusion of certain oral forms must be added a concern for the processes by which oral traditions engage events in history and existential events, so that their performance amounts to a meaningful application of traditional forms to particular felt concerns.

Perhaps our notions about oral traditions have been overly shaped by a literal reading of the stories, for they often open with phrases like "In the beginning" or "In the time when the ancestors and gods lived on the earth." We have linked this primal setting with the stock response given when a person of a nonliterate culture is asked if he makes up or creates the stories he tells: "How can stories which tell of the creation of the world and of human life, stories which tell of the ancestors and gods be made up?" We then conclude that oral traditions, particularly stories of origin, are of great antiquity and pass through the history of a culture, or from culture to culture, virtually unchanged. But on this point I think we have perhaps acted hastily and have looked too superficially at the stories, particularly since they are oral in form.

In order to reexamine the idea of the history and change of oral traditions, let us look at the story of Hainuwele, especially as recently discussed by Jonathan Z. Smith.[3] The story of Hainuwele was first recorded in 1927 from the people of West Ceram, an island west of New Guinea. It received little attention until Adolf Jensen recorded several versions of it in 1937 and 1938 and subsequently devoted a number of articles to its interpretation. It has since become one of the most studied of stories, and as Jonathan Smith notes, a consensus recognizes it as having great antiquity, its principal concern being the presentation of the origins of human death, sexuality, and cultivated food plants. Upon a brief summary of the story we can review the interpretation offered by Smith, for it helps us to understand the processes by which oral traditions address the contemporary needs of a people.

In the beginning, nine families left Mount Nunusaku, where they had emerged from clusters of bananas, and migrated to West Ceram. While hunting one day a man named Ameta found a wild boar who had drowned in a lake. On the boar's tusk was stuck a coconut. Ameta took home the coconut, a thing then unknown, and in his dreams that night a figure appeared and instructed him to plant the coconut. Ameta did so the next morning. In just a few days the coconut had grown into a tall palm and had begun to bloom. Ameta, thinking to make a

---

[3] Jonathan Z. Smith, "A Pearl of Great Price and a Cargo of Yams: A Study in Situational Incongruity," *History of Religions*, Vol. 16, No. 1 (1976), 1–19. The discussion here of the Hainuwele story is largely based on this article.

drink from the flowers, climbed the tree to harvest them, but in the process he slashed his finger and the blood dropped upon a blossom. Returning several days later, Ameta found in place of this blossom a girl whom he named Hainuwele (coconut girl), and he took her home with him. She was no ordinary girl for when, as the English translation puts it, "she answered the call of nature," she excreted valuable articles which made Ameta very rich.

Soon a festival was celebrated. It was customary for the women to sit in the center of the dance ground and distribute betel nuts to the men as they danced about them in spirals. On this occasion, Hainuwele took her place in the center of the dance ground. On the first day she passed out betel nuts, but when the men asked her, she gave them the things which she could excrete. Each day after that she gave them something bigger and more valuable: coral, porcelain dishes, bush knives, copper boxes, golden earrings, and glorious gongs.

As the festival approached its final day, the people began to think that what Hainuwele was doing was mysterious, and they decided to kill her. They dug a pit in the center of the dance ground, and as the dancers approached Hainuwele, they pushed her in the pit, covered her over, and danced the dirt firmly down.

Ameta soon missed Hainuwele and went in search of her. After he found and exhumed her dead body, he cut it into pieces which he reburied around the village. These pieces grew into the various tuberous plants, giving origin to the principal foods which these people have enjoyed ever since.[4]

Interpretations of this story usually recall that it is set "in the beginning" and makes reference to the origin of sexuality, human death, and tuberous foods. But if we follow our own senses, we can scarcely avoid thinking that what is most striking about the story is what Hainuwele produces and how she produces it. It is with a focus on this point that Smith reexamines the story. He suspends the assumption that the story reports incidents only of great antiquity, so that he might discover to what extent it can be considered a response to the historical and cultural situation of the West Ceramese at the time the story was recorded. In other words, Smith holds that while the story is a part of an oral tradition having some considerable historical depth, the version recorded in 1937 had been adapted in such a way as to respond directly to the felt needs of the culture at that time. We must know the background of the situation in West Ceram in the first three decades of this century to provide the context for interpreting the story in this way.

In New Guinea and Melanesia the traditional system of values centered on the idea of equivalence. No individual or family maintained more or less goods and food stuffs than any other. Ceremonies and feasts accompanied the end of harvest so as to consume inequities in production, thus assuring equivalences among the community. Personal wealth and prestige were measured neither by

---

[4] The source for the English translation of the Hainuwele story is Joseph Campbell, *The Masks of God: Primitive Mythology* (New York, Viking Press, 1959), pp. 173–76.

quantities of goods produced or acquired nor by the thrift and resourcefulness which may result in such quantities. Rather, prestige was measured, in part, by one's skill in achieving reciprocity, by giving in proportion to what one received, so as to remain equivalent to everyone else.

When European goods and money were introduced into this situation they precipitated a crisis of a fundamental sort because they challenged the very worth of human life for the native peoples. Reciprocity and the resulting equivalence were clearly impossible to obtain because the native peoples had little access to the European goods. They could not make them, and they could not make the Europeans understand the importance of their system of reciprocity and equivalences.

With this as general background, Smith notes that the area of West Ceram was intensively colonized by the Dutch beginning in the period 1902–1910. The treatment of the people native to West Ceram included the suppression of their traditions by the destruction of community houses and the imposition of a tax to be paid in cash or its equivalent in work. Given this heightened situation of incongruity, Smith argues that the story of Hainuwele as recorded arose during this period as a response to the incongruities colonization had introduced. The response, although uniquely developed for the particular situation, is rooted in the West Ceramese tradition. The story of Hainuwele is related to stories recorded earlier of Yam Woman, who also produced food by mysterious means. In these stories the situation was resolved by killing Yam Woman and eating the food she produced. In the story of Hainuwele, according to Smith's interpretation, the Yam Woman has been developed into a figure who presents the incongruity of colonization, a figure who mysteriously produced foreign goods—knives, dishes, and gongs. The incongruity which this situation creates is resolved in the story by cannibalism, the traditional way that something external and threatening can be incorporated, that is, by murdering and eating it. In this view, Hainuwele is a story whose roots in oral traditions may well have great antiquity, but as recorded it represents an application of the tradition in an attempt to resolve the incongruity of the presence of Europeans and their goods.

Clearly the story did not resolve the situation. It did not dispense with the Europeans nor their goods. It did not even give the native peoples access to the manufacture of the goods. It did not change the value system of either party. But through the language of the story, which gave the situation a place in primordial reality, it permitted the crisis to be directly addressed; it encompassed the situation into the language and thought of the people and thereby supported the hope that it might be resolved.

Through this example we may further appreciate the vitality with which oral traditions can serve the presently felt needs of a people while maintaining a tradition through time. It is an attribute inseparable from the inherent aspect of oral traditions. To speak to current issues by way of the stories of origin is to address them in perhaps the most powerful way available.

THE ETERNAL RENEWAL OF ORAL TRADITIONS

To this point in our consideration of oral traditions we have emphasized two aspects which are in tension. On the one hand, oral traditions embody something that is stable, definable, formal, and not subject to much change or alteration. Yet on the other hand, and this point we have emphasized perhaps more heavily, oral traditions are performed and gain their life and vitality, indeed their meaning, from the response they make to specific cultural situations, both historical and existential. It seems to me that the defining character of oral traditions is bound up in this tension and that it would clarify our endeavor to discuss this point from yet another perspective.

The seminal works of Mircea Eliade have opened our eyes to the regular patterns which flow through so much of the history of human religiousness. One of the most remarkable patterns Eliade has shown us is what he has called "the myth of the eternal return." It has served greatly to liberate us from certain expectations about religion which have been fostered by Western religious history.

Focusing especially on stories of creation and recognizing the reflection of the cosmic structures revealed in art and architecture, rite and drama, Eliade has shown the archetypes and models which are characteristic of archaic and nonliterate peoples. These models are established in the stories of creation, stories which tell of a time "in the beginning" when creator gods, heroes, and divine ancestors lived. The stories tell how the present world came to be, and they recount how the primordial figures established the way human life should be lived. These stories therefore are sacred and true because they recount the acts of primordial figures who are not confined to this world.

Eliade has shown that in the periodic recitation and ritual enactment of these stories, the events of the stories are repeated. Such ritual acts result in the periodic re-creation and renewal of the world itself. From these observations, Eliade concludes that archaic and nonliterate peoples tolerate history, the events of time, rather reluctantly as shown by their need to periodically turn to the renewal or re-creation of the world. In Eliade's view these peoples refuse to accept themselves as historical beings and refuse to grant value to events in history. In their eternal return to the primal paradise of pristine creation, a reality is gained which is uncontaminated by time and becoming. Hence, the degree to which one lives according to the archaic models held in the stories is the degree to which life is meaningful, is real, is religious. In a sense, as Eliade says, nothing new ever happens in a life lived according to the pattern of the eternal return.[5]

_____

[5] Mircea Eliade, *Cosmos and History: The Myth of the Eternal Return* (New York: Harper & Row, Publishers, Inc., 1959), especially Chapter 2; and *The Sacred and the Profane* (New York: Harper & Row, Publishers, Inc., 1959), especially Chapter 2.

Set against the common Western view that time is an irreversible linear succession of historical moments, this notion is greatly liberating. Eliade introduces us to the idea that time is not irreversible. Time can be renewed through regeneration by the repetition of the archaic models of creation. But there is a problem here also, for the myth of the eternal return is clearest only when set as a foil against this linear notion of historical time. The very language of the eternal return is the language of historical time and finally contradicts itself. If the reality fostered by the eternal return is an eternal present with no past or future, what then does one mean by return? If the motivation for the return is a reaction against the chaos or meaninglessness of history, then this element of chaos is essential to the process. These contradictions and tensions are resolved by bending the time line upon itself into a closed circle of repetitions, so that every past is a future and every future a past. Yet this representation not only rejects history, innovation, and change; it also rejects the very nature of time itself. Hence, Eliade concludes that "like the mystic, like the religious man in general, the primitive lives in a continual present."[6]

Perhaps if we can extricate ourselves from thinking of time as unidimensional, as a succession of moments which may be, at any present, divided into past and future, we may be able to see another dimension of Eliade's pattern which will be especially valuable for us. Certainly, both the past and the future have some present reality in terms of our memory and future expectations. We can see these divisions of time present in the Akan dirges. The central theme involves the ancestors, people of past generations who have died and are no longer among the living, but who nevertheless remain important in the present because of the role they play in bringing about the future. The presence of death is an occasion for anguish only because of its nonrepetitive and irreversible character. The dead are prepared for their future existence in another world, yet their past lives are remembered and honored.

What I am suggesting is that we may see the processes of oral traditions more clearly as reapplication and renewal of the forms whose historical roots may be ancient. In the recitation of the stories, the experiences of concrete time, of history, are digested so that the sanctioning description of reality in the oral traditions corresponds with and interprets the lived experience of reality. Certainly not everything experienced in history is given positive value, but it must be part of the story to even be rejected as dirt or excrement. The story of Hainuwele can be seen as a description of the process of digesting and excreting the facts of historical experience, thus renewing the tradition in light of present needs and history. The historical experience of the incongruity brought on by the colonial situation is digested by the people into the story of Hainuwele, which uniquely responds to the archetypes of tradition and to the present experience even when incongruous by conferring primordial status upon the present. The

---

[6] Eliade, *Cosmos and History,* p. 86.

past and future are not the same; there is no eternal present lived in a shroud of mystery. Rather the models of the past are brought to bear upon the present situation so as to spawn future-oriented motivations and expectations in the present. We need not think of this process in the metaphorical terms of either circles or lines.

I don't think this view is really at odds with the pattern Eliade has discerned, because he observes that the stories of origins have their own histories and that they are the last stage of development, not the first. In other words, he recognizes that oral traditions come about and live by historical processes which use the events of time as raw materials. History is transfigured into story and made real on the one hand while being interpreted and given meaning by it on the other. He notes that memory of historical events is modified so that only that which is patterned in the sacred models is preserved after a time. But often this time is long, even as much as two or three centuries when carried in such forms as epic poetry.

At this point we must recall that differing modes of communication have a significant effect on culture and the ways in which it is transmitted. The retention of the historicity of any event for a period of even one or two centuries without the aid of writing is remarkable and attests to an intense interest in history or to the admitted impact of certain events in history. This point is even more striking in light of the fact that for most nonliterate peoples throughout human history, the average life expectancy has been remarkably short. Given the constraints and freedoms which accompany different modes of communication, I would suggest that a certain degree of antihistoricity is inseparable from the oral mode in terms of simple physical and mental constraints. Yet the accompanying freedom gained by the finitude of retained historical data permits the maintenance of an integrated body of stories which may constantly develop by an organic process of digesting history and forgetting things that cease to be relevant. Through the story the past and future live in the present. Little wonder that many nonliterate peoples think of their stories as persons.

Surely we can no longer justify the sharp division we have so commonly made between ourselves as historically inclined and nonliterate peoples as ahistorical. We can no longer picture ourselves as self-consciously living in a stream of history with a sense of the sharp distinction between the past and the future in contrast to nonliterate peoples living in the mystical timelessness of their fanciful stories and tales.

TYPES OF ORAL TRADITIONS

Beginning with the collection of folktales by Jakob and Wilhelm Grimm in the 19th century, there has been a proliferation of classifications and types into which these data are sorted. I have avoided this subject as long as I dare, and I have ignored what differences in type might exist between, for example, a dirge and a story of cosmic origin. Certainly there are classifications and types of oral material, and we need to consider them, but it is not easy to give a very clear picture of this breakdown. First, we must remember that the terms we use are all rooted in Western languages and applied by Western scholars to their data. Then we must remember that there have been many fields of scholarship making use of these terms—folklore, ethnology, anthropology, literature, and religion—and within each of these fields there are many conflicting schools of thought. The consequence is that rarely do we find standard usage of terms within one field, much less among them all. What one field calls a tale, another calls a myth; what for one is oral literature is for another folklore; and so on. Where avowed truth and subject matter are the criteria for classification by some, it is frequency and type of transmission by another. A considerable amount of scholarly effort has been expended on these classification schemes, and raging controversies frequently erupt—rightly so, since these fields of study are shaped in part by how they classify and value the data of oral traditions. I do not think it productive to enter the arena to offer yet another scheme, but rather, after discussing the usage of a term whose use has been particularly confusing, I will argue against the importance of such schemes altogether for the purpose of determining what is and is not relevant to the study of religion.

There is one term so commonly, yet so variously, used that it would be irresponsible not to discuss it, and that term is *myth.* I have already had to use it in discussing Eliade's idea of the "myth of the eternal return." In common English usage, myth denotes a false belief or an untrue, often fanciful, story. This usage stems from the Greek *mythos,* which denotes "word" in the sense of a final pronouncement, but contrasts with *logos,* which denotes "word" whose validity or truth can be argued and demonstrated. However, in the modern use of the term by religion scholars, it is the truth of myth which distinguishes it. Myths, as commonly described, are narrative accounts of the gods in a time that is altogether different from that of ordinary human experience. Such narratives are recognized as an essential constituent of religion and of human culture. The truth of these narratives is self-evident in their human context, for the world which resulted from the remarkable acts of the gods is none other than the one observed. Because of the view that myths present a model for human behavior which is authoritative because its source and subject transcend ordinary human reality, religion scholars have concentrated their attention on mythology to the near exclusion of folklore, legends, jokes, sagas, fables, epics, songs, and even prayer. Most of the study of religion, we must note, has not considered any form of oral expression at all but has rather dealt exclusively with sacred scriptures and intellectual interpretive writings.

I do not want to deny the importance of myth as a subject of study, but I think to limit one's data to such a classification, however it is defined, is to limit radically the potential of one's understanding. Ruth Finnegan, a student of African oral traditions, finds relatively little in Africa that could in a strict sense be called mythology, yet African cultures are rich in oral traditions.[7] We would not want to ignore African cultures or suggest on the basis of this lack of mythology that they have no religions. Further, if we ignore folklore because entertainment is one of its outstanding features, if we ignore jokes because of their lightness or seemingly base character, if we ignore fables because they are fictitious, it seems to me we ignore much that is of great value in understanding the religious world views of any people we study.

Perhaps of greater importance than the classifications we give to oral traditions are those given by the people to their own oral forms. Such native classification is common. The importance of these indigenous categories is not so much to help us find which parts of oral traditions are without value for our study, but rather so that we may know how the culture defines and values its own categories. To know what is thought false, what is dirt, what is forbidden is often very illuminating, as the story of Hainuwele has shown and as we will see again. Knowing such distinctions may be as important as knowing what is held to be true and authoritative.

THE NYANGA ORAL TRADITIONS

At this point it may appear that performances of oral traditions are confined to special occasions, such as funerals, festivals, entertainment events. Certainly, these are common occasions for oral performances, but it is essential that we appreciate the degree to which oral traditions permeate culture. For most nonliterate peoples it would be a rare day that did not call for several kinds of oral performance.

Let us look at the oral traditions of the Nyanga, a Bantu-speaking people in Zaire. These people live in a mountainous rain forest. Their most significant economic activity is trapping, but they also engage in gathering, hunting, and fishing, and they grow such crops as bananas, grains, and roots. The technology to support these activities is quite limited, yet what exists is highly efficient.

Daniel Biebuyck gives us a rich account of Nyanga oral traditions and their cultural contents.[8] Engagement in oral traditions is nearly a constant affair for the Nyanga. Every day, after returning from their work in the forest, groups of men meet to eat, relax, discuss the affairs of the day, and plan for the next. These meetings, which may last well into the evening, are the occasions for frequent telling of tales, proverbs, and riddles. Biebuyck says that these forms of

---

[7] Ruth Finnegan, *Oral Literature in Africa* (Oxford: Oxford University Press, 1970), pp. 361–67.

[8] Daniel Biebuyck and Kahombo C. Mateene, eds. and trans., *The Mwindo Epic* (Berkeley: University of California Press, 1969). The discussion here is based on materials presented in this book.

FIGURE 5.1. A Gealeka storyteller of the Transkei (Africa). (From *The Xhosa Ntsomi* by Harold Scheub, published by © Oxford University Press, 1975. Used by permission.)

oral tradition are not simply to entertain but to clarify ideas, interpret events, and enhance values. The women too use a wide range of oral forms in their daily domestic routines of food preparation and child rearing. Biebuyck says that the same stories may be used by both men and women, but often their conclusions or what explanations or values they serve are different. Adolescents also meet on a daily basis to dance and play games making use of various oral forms. Oral performances are often accompanied by hand clapping and singing or musical instruments ranging from drums and percussion sticks to antelope horns, flutes, calabash rattles, and zithers. For the Nyanga, as for most nonliterate peoples, oral traditions are commonplace in culture. They provide the forms and structures through which conversation, daily activities, teaching, and decision making take place. They bear the values as well as the processes of culture.

In this case we find our understanding and appreciation enriched by the Nyanga classifications of their oral forms made available by Biebuyck's remarkable attentiveness. A quick review will help us see the extent and variation which oral forms can take.

- **Mushumo** is a category of terse sayings, like proverbs, which are poetic in form and which represent Nyanga values. When performed often only the first phrase is given, and the audience is engaged to provide the completion. They are used on all occasions of instruction but most especially during initiations.

- **Inondo** refers to riddles in poetic form which may be recited or sung, most usually by women and adolescents.

- **Mubikiriro** are prayers in poetic form which men slowly recite without musical accompaniment, pausing between phrases to permit auditors' comments. Many are the occasions and motivations for prayer.

- State occasions are times for eulogistic recitations (**musinjo**) honoring chiefs and headmen. The performance is by men, delivered in a highly rhythmic staccato manner unaccompanied by music. The eulogies consist mainly of names associated with the history of the people.

- **Ihamurivo** are stereotyped formulas used by diviners and medicine men. They have esoteric aspects and are recited extremely rapidly.

- **Rwimbo** are songs which are commonly composed by stringing together proverbs. The context of their performance greatly shapes the meaning and point to which they are directed. Songs appear in many situations and occur within other oral forms like tales and epics.

- Tales fall into two categories, depending on whether they have a supernatural element (**uano**) or not (**mushinga**), and their range and number are very great. They usually focus on an animal character, although human beings, divinities, celestial bodies, and abstract figures do appear. The performance of tales is open to anybody and may include song, mime, and dramatization. Most tales have a mixture of roles, including education, explanation, recreation, and moralization. The specific situation and nature of the performance give emphasis to one or more of these.

- Trappers and hunters are the experts at telling **nganuriro** or "true stories," which center on anecdotes, adventures, or unusual powers or skills that the teller or his close relative possesses.

- **Mwanikiro** are meditations and reflections expressed in a concise style. These often provide material for songs.

- Headmen, chiefs, and elders may state their views in well-wrought and systematic discourses (**kishambaro**).

- **Ihano** refers to instructions made to youth about their culture. They amount to concise stereotyped descriptions of the rules of behavior for the culture.

- Doubtless the most magnificent of oral forms is the epic (**karisi**). These long poems are known by only a few men and they are performed mainly on special request.

More needs to be said about *karisi*, but first we should reflect on the significance of these many categories of oral tradition. We see that the Nyanga have a rich variety of oral forms of expression, and their linguistic differentiation shows that they are fully aware of these forms and their differences. Each type is defined by the Nyanga in terms of its content, its occasion for performance, its style of performance, and its performer. Taken all together we can see that for the Nyanga their oral traditions are a constant presence serving to maintain cultural continuity (tradition) through a history of change and development.

Turning now to the Nyanga epics, we have an opportunity to appreciate still further the aspects of creativity and performance in the oral traditions of a nonliterate people. All Nyanga know some parts of their oral traditions, but not all members of the culture are as talented at performing as others. Some few stand out in any village as superior performers of one oral form or another. However, the epic narratives require yet far greater skills.

The name *karisi* denotes the epic narrative and performance for most Nyanga, but for the bard it denotes a male spirit as well. It is this spirit figure who appears to the bard in a dream and implores him to devote himself to *karisi*, both spirit and narrative. The bard does so by learning and performing the epic *karisi* and by presenting offerings of banana beer to the spirit *karisi* at a special shrine. As a consequence the bards call themselves *karisi*. This identity of bard, narrative, and spirit opens to us the religious significance which the performance of the epic has for the bard. He believes that the proper performance will make him strong and impervious to disease and death. He finds in his performance the strength that is possessed by the culture hero, Mwindo.

The epic focuses on the adventures of Mwindo, who is human in form but most remarkable in every way. He was not conceived and born as a normal human, though his parents are human. Small in stature, Mwindo has many special gifts which permit him modes of travel through water, underground, and on land. He also has the gift of premonition, and he holds magical objects which give him the means for magical escape from the worst imaginable difficulties. He has many powerful friends, human, animal, and supernatural. He is bent upon the destruction of evil and the rescue of people. He fights and slays a fierce dragon from whose body he rescues many people—a thousand people from each of the dragon's eyes. He is cast off into space to suffer unbearable heat and cold without help or protection. In every sense he is a true superhero.

The whole epic is never performed at one time—indeed there is a sense in which it never could be complete and finished—but selected episodes are performed at the request of a headman or chief for any who wish to attend. Biebuyck has recorded from a remarkable bard a very extensive version of the epic which runs over one hundred printed pages in its English translation. The style of performance is quite complex. Each episode is first sung and then narrated, and both styles of performance are supported with musical accompaniment, dance, mime, and dramatization performed by a group practiced in epic accompaniment as well as by the whole audience. The bard may receive small gifts and high praise for his performance, and beer and food are enjoyed by all.

Although the action of the epic is set in the remote past, the space in which it takes place spans every one of the divisions of cosmos and earth recognized by the Nyanga. In its content and performance, the Mwindo epic presents all the features that define and characterize Nyanga culture and religion. It portrays customs, behavior patterns, values, economic activities, and material objects. It presents the origin and history of certain institutions. In its performance it also utilizes nearly all oral forms of expression. In short, as Biebuyck notes, it is a synopsis of Nyanga culture.

Once again it is notable that although there are clearly constraints on the epic form and content, the narrator may exercise considerable personal creativity in the selection of episodes, the enhancement of content, and most certainly in the dramatic performance. To become an epic bard is a tremendous accomplishment for any human being because one must learn the epic not only as song and poetry but also as dance and drama. To master such a task is not unique to the few Nyanga epic bards, but regularly occurs among nonliterate peoples all over the world. Geneologies extending to one hundred generations have been recorded among the Kwakiutl in North America. Song and prayer cycles sung in sequence throughout a period of nine days and nights are common performances by Navajo medicine men. Biebuyck recorded from one Nyanga man 21 very long tales, 82 "true" stories, 43 interpretations of dreams, 268 riddles, and 327 songs. We must become fully aware that oral traditions are commonly very extensive, complex in form, and sophisticated and imaginative in thought, content, and style. But even more important to our concern, much can be learned of religious thought and belief from a careful study of oral traditions. As we have seen, religion could scarcely be separated from oral traditions; at many points they are indistinguishable.

THE TRICKSTER

We have considered several examples of oral traditions which have been primarily formal and serious. Yet I have constantly stressed the importance of considering those forms of oral traditions which appear to be lighter and obviously entertaining. To illustrate something of this importance we will now discuss one of the most fascinating, but also most widely misunderstood, figures in oral traditions. He has come to be called the *trickster.* This figure, distinguished perhaps most of all by his defiance of any definition or restriction, appears in many forms—animal, human, and indeterminate forms—in the tales of many nonliterate peoples the world over. To give the trickster some presence here we must tell a few stories. All of them have been selected from the Apache in the American Southwest.

Coyote Strikes His Forked Hat

Coyote was taking a nap. He woke up. He forgot that he had a forked hat. He had put it on his knee when he fell asleep.

He woke up and saw the hat on his knee. He thought it was the head of some animal playing a joke on him. He thought the forked ends were the ears. He made believe that he didn't see it. He closed his eyes again and put his hand back and felt for a stone. When he found one, he put his arm behind his head and then stretched. He opened his eyes just a little and brought the stone down on the hat. It hit his own leg. It made a cracking noise, as though a board were hit.

"Oh, I've done things like this many times!" he cried. "I've hit my own leg!"[9]

Coyote Causes Death

Raven said that he didn't want death in this world. "I'll throw a stick in the river. If it sinks there is going to be death, but if not, everything will be all right," he said.

Then Coyote came along and said, "I'll throw a rock in the river. If it sinks people will die. If it doesn't sink there will be no death."

Raven threw the sticks and they floated off. Then Coyote threw the rock and it sank. After that people began to die off.[10]

Coyote Makes Woman Valuable by Breaking the Teeth in Her Vagina

One time Coyote found a very pretty woman. He tried to make love to her. He took her in the woods on a walk. He wanted to have intercourse with her and was just about to do so when he saw teeth in her vagina. He was afraid. When she wasn't looking he got a stick and a long slender rock.

First, instead of putting his penis in, he put in the stick, and it was ground up. Then he put the rock in, and the teeth were knocked off until her vagina became just as a woman's is now. After that he had intercourse with her.

Then the woman said, "Hereafter I shall be worth a lot. I am worth horses and many things now."

That is why men give horses and different things when they marry women today.[11]

How Coyote First Made Bows and Arrows

Coyote went to the wild mulberry bush. He said to it, "I want to make a bow. The people who come after me will make it as I do."

He got the wood. He cut it off with flint. He split it. Then he whittled it into a bow shape. He didn't fix it right away. He took it back and seasoned it.

Then he went to another bush called "yellow berry." It doesn't grow here but in the southern part of Texas. It has little yellow berries.

To this bush he said, "I'd like some of your wood to make arrows so that after this the people can make them as I do."

Then he went to a turkey. He asked the turkey for a favor.

"What is it?" asked the turkey.

"I'd like to have some feathers."

"Why?"

"To feather my arrows."

He had all these things. He came back to camp. He had some sinew. He twisted it and made a bow string. "Now the people who come after me will use it the way I do." he said.

[9] Morris E. Opler, *Myths and Legends of the Lipan Apache Indians* (New York: J. J. Augustin Publisher, 1940), pp. 192–93.

[10] Morris E. Opler, *Myths and Tales of the Chiricahua Apache Indians,* Memoirs of the American Folk-lore Society, Vol. 37 (1942), p. 28.

[11] *Ibid.,* p. 70.

Now he had them all finished.

There is one who lives above the clouds. They call him Wise One. Coyote spoke to him. He said, "Make a little groove in my arrow."

This one replied, "This is the way you want those." He made three grooves on the shafts. "Some will be straight and some zigzag," he told Coyote. "The zigzag will stand for the lightning."[12]

Doubtless the entertainment value of these stories draws our first reaction. We are not at odds here with the way tales of the trickster, in these stories Coyote, are understood by the people who tell and hear them. Usually the cycle of stories about the trickster are well known by all and thoroughly enjoyed with every retelling. The most common occasion for the telling of these stories is one when entertainment seems to be the primary concern. The trickster's pranks are imaginative; his eroticism is gross; his blunders are devastating. But there is a pitfall in embracing only the entertainment value of the trickster tales, for we are conditioned to think that what is fun and entertaining cannot also be serious and profound. Consequently, far too many scholars have simply ignored these tales or have set them aside from any serious consideration by labeling them "just entertainment." We must avoid this pitfall. I have come to appreciate especially one thing about the trickster: He is never quite what you think he is. He'll never do what you expect him to do. So I must warn you that as I discuss the Apache stories to try to show what the trickster is, it is his nature not to conform to any definition we give him.

As we review the figure of Coyote in these four short tales, we may be struck by how different he appears from one story to the next. In one he is a foolish buffoon who can't tell his hat from the head of some animal. As the bringer of death, he is still foolish in his actions, but the consequence of his rash action is suffered by all of humanity. In contrast, Coyote's affair with the toothed vagina, which is a widespread image in folklore, has its comic erotic elements, but its result makes possible procreation, pleasure in sexuality, and the cultural practices of giving gifts for a bride. Here the results of Coyote's adventure are positive in human experience, as they are in the story in which Coyote introduces bows and arrows for human use.

From these brief examples we begin to see that the simplistic and base appearance of the trickster belies a more complex character whose role is ultimately in service to the definition of a culture and its ways.

In a study of North American tricksters, Mac L. Ricketts has shown that the figure we call trickster is a complex one composed of prankster, transformer, and culture hero.[13] As prankster he sets his wits and strengths against all others in an attempt to show his superiority. Sometimes his tricks are successful, as in

[12] Opler, *Myths and Legends of the Lipan Apache*, p. 115.

[13] Mac L. Ricketts, "The North American Indian Trickster," *History of Religions*, Vol. 5, No. 2 (1966), 327–50. See also the important recent work of Robert Pelton, *The Trickster in West Africa* (Berkeley: University of California Press, 1980).

the Apache story in which he shams the killing of a monster so that he may appear to be brave and heroic. Sometimes they seem exceedingly cruel, as in the Apache story in which Coyote takes advantage of two old blind women by provoking them to fight each other and by causing them to be drowned by moving the rope which guided them to water. But commonly his tricks backfire, and he suffers the consequences of embarrassment, physical pain, and even death. If we look at the prankster, we find reflected in him the weaknesses and strengths which are distinctive of human nature. Human beings are driven by basic needs such as food and sex. The trickster will do virtually anything for a meal. In one Apache story he eats forbidden berries and has trouble keeping his feet on the ground because of his expulsion of intestinal gas which the berries created. The trickster is grossly erotic and his sexual needs are insatiable. Few Apache stories of Coyote are without this element. For example, he goes so far in satisfying his sexual needs that he sleeps with his mother-in-law and marries his daughter. But like human beings, the trickster is persistent and does not let failures of any kind discourage him. He learns, but slowly, by his mistakes. In an Apache story Coyote spends a whole day chopping down trees to try to capture a turkey, but as each tree begins to fall, the turkey simply flies to another.

The trickster is also a transformer, as in the examples of the bringer of death and the fixer of the toothed vagina. Here he plays a role alongside the creator gods and ancestors. In fact, the trickster is often portrayed in the role of antagonist to creation, undoing some of its elements. But the effect is to set the order of things as they are experienced in human reality. People die and rivers run only downstream. The trickster in his transforming acts is defining reality.

The trickster can put aside the role of prankster and transformer and be a culture hero by serving directly the needs of humanity even at the risk of his own life and limb. Here he is altruistic, selfless, wise, and thoughtful. He removes obstacles from human life and helps to protect human beings from pain and distress. He introduces culture into nature as in the manufacture of bows and arrows.

In sum, although the trickster participates in the cosmic design, he is not a god or supernatural figure. His accomplishments are often due to his folly, which may be seen as the source of his wisdom. He tests the character of humanity at its very limits, and it is because he has the courage or the drive to go to these limits that he reveals so much about the nature of the world and humanity. This factor also makes him a figure essential to religion. The reason the trickster cannot be defined is that it is his nature to test definition by violating its limits. The trickster is the very embodiment of humor. When people laugh at him they find a way to laugh at themselves, at their own limitations and foolishness. This insight permits human beings to live with the burden of the failures and limitations which are part of human nature, yet to realize that these very constraints are part of the process of gaining self-transcendence, part of the process of coming to know the aspects of reality which are beyond human failures and limitations.

CONCLUSION

In this discussion of oral traditions in nonliterate cultures we have pointed out several factors which establish a kind of tension in which oral traditions gain their definitive character. This defining tension is, it seems to me, captured in the very term, *oral traditions*. The word *oral* suggests to us an act of the mouth and the heart, an act of spontaneity and creativity, an act of life and breath, an act of freedom and emotion, an act of the living individual in a human community. The word *traditions* suggests to us formality, history, sameness, continuity, and group sanction. It is in the tension suggested by the words that oral traditions serve cultures, and particularly their religious dimensions.

The forms which traditions take, both in terms of content and performance, when manifest orally, must be appreciated. They serve to convey messages appropriate to the needs that motivate them, and they also serve symbolically to set the proper moods and emotions for the occasion. But we must be careful not to misjudge the often formulaic character of oral traditions as a deterrent to their vitality, a stagnation into wooden repetition. This formal character serves as a channel through which flows lively and creative expression.

In their richness and variety, in their types and functions, we can also appreciate how oral traditions are pervasive in nonliterate cultures. They permeate every corner of human life. When taken as a whole, these variously suited types amount to an affecting presence. That is, in total they constitute an ever-present culture-defining, orienting, and value-maintaining milieu. Oral traditions are the means and media of culture. They serve to mold people into the patterns of culture by instructing them, restricting them, and defining their activities and goals. Yet they also serve as the means by which people bring about changes in their culture. Oral traditions enable the people to respond to and adapt to changes in the environment and in their relations with others. It is through oral forms that cultures obtain their history and transform their code of values. It is without question that oral traditions are vital to our understanding of the religions of nonliterate peoples.

ritual

As we parked the car along the side of a dusty road and turned off the engine, we could hear them coming. *Clack, jingle, clack, jingle.* In the quiet village the air was electric with anticipation as we hurried with others through the dry midmorning July heat at Hotevilla to climb a ladder to the pueblo rooftop overlooking the dance plaza. Getting settled, we could hear them approaching. *Clack, jingle, clack, jingle.* Emerging from the tunnel-like opening between two pueblos the kachinas entered the plaza. Hopi women and children and visitors from other villages were still taking their places on wooden benches and folding chairs around the plaza edge and on the surrounding rooftops. The brilliantly colorful costumes of the kachinas were a striking contrast to the brown of the dirt plaza and the adobe buildings.

The occasion was Niman, the last time the kachinas would be seen that year. Since the winter solstice they had been among the Hopi people, bringing them life in the form of nurturing rain for the corn plants. In their appearances in *kiva* and plaza dances, the kachinas, with the clowns, had shown what it is to be Hopi; they had revealed and celebrated the Hopi way of life. Now that the corn was nearing maturity, assuring the continuance of life for the year ahead, it was time for them to return to their homes in the San Francisco mountains, whose snow-capped peaks some ninety miles to the west can be seen from the Hopi mesas. The Niman ceremony is their farewell, and it is made without the clowns. The solemnity of the occasion seemed to heighten the awesome beauty of the *angak'china,* or long-hair kachina.

Each carried green corn stalks or cattails and fruit and gifts of kachina dolls or miniature bows and arrows as they filed into the plaza. They laid these things in the plaza center and took their places in a line extending along one side and end of the plaza. As they prepared to sing and dance, the impeccable detail of their appearance was stunning. Adorning the slender hard bodies of youth and the massive torsos of middle-aged men, the costumes were uniform in appearance. The face portion of the long-hair kachina mask is turquoise and is set on long black hair hanging straight from the crown of the head midway down chest and back. Three downy breath feathers are attached to the face. Downy feathers adorn a cotton cord hanging from the crown of the head down the back of the hair. Attached to the end of the cord is a shell or small woven plaque. On top of the head is a tuft of yellow downy feathers in conjunction with a single long macaw feather of brilliant color which extends vertically well above the head.

Clay markings are worn on the naked upper body. A white woven kilt is bound by a wide and a narrow sash. The wide one is unbleached fiber, the ends of which hang down the right side, and is beautifully embroidered in green, red, and blue designs. The narrow sash is woven red, black, and green. A fox pelt hangs in back from the sash with its tail nearing the ground. Spruce boughs are placed around the sash at the waist. A turtle shell rattle is worn on the right calf and a band of sleigh bells on the left. Turquoise moccasins are worn. A gourd rattle is carried in the right hand and a spruce bough in the left. Turquoise bracelets, necklaces, and decorated bow guards are also worn.

Passing along the line of dancers, the kachina fathers, plainly dressed elders, bless the kachinas by sprinkling their shoulders with cornmeal. *Clack, clack.* The head kachina sets the rhythm with his right foot, and as the others pick up the beat, the song wells up to fill the plaza. It is a sound I cannot describe. The thought of it always evokes in me the feelings it inspired, feelings which are

FIGURE 6.1. Hopi long-hair kachina dolls. (Courtesy Heard Museum, Phoenix, Arizona.)

somehow so deep and so moving that they are no easier to describe than is the sonorous music. The dance is stately and orderly, a stepping in place, but with turns and a complex rhythm. The perfection of the costume, the dance, and the song is awesome. It evokes a power that is undeniable even to the outsider who has no knowledge of what is going on.

If we ask a Hopi what this is all about we would doubtless be told on this occasion that it is "the home dance," that is, the farewell dance the kachinas do before they return to their home. If we press the issue and ask more generally why do kachinas come to Hopi and dance, we will be told simply that "they dance for rain" or that Niman turns the sun back in its course.

Becoming interested in Hopi ritual, we consult ethnographies and attend more Hopi dances, and we are soon overwhelmed by the complexity and elaborateness of these ritual performances. We find that what we see at Niman is just a single tiny facet of a large and brilliant jewel. As we look at one facet we are drawn to, and even see reflections of, its many other facets. We realize that although we are arrested by the surface, we can catch glimpses of the secret of the deep beauty of the jewel, a beauty whose source we can never fully grasp.

Niman is a nine-day ceremony composed of many ritual acts performed mostly in the privacy of *kivas*. The dances on the last two days are a public conclusion to this ceremony. It is only one of many such ceremonies performed during the kachina season, which unfolds during half of the year. Other kinds of dances and ceremonies occur during the other half. It doesn't take long to begin to see the complexity of any of these ceremonies, for each involves extensive knowledge and an immense effort to perform.

However, in any attempt to understand these rituals, we are faced with peculiarities which are inseparable from the very nature of ritual. We know that distinctive to the character of ritual is its regularity, sameness, formality, and rigidity; yet we are often told by its performers of its creativity as well as of the effects it has on the world. This aspect leads us to the difficult problems of trying to understand ritual, not only in this Hopi setting, but also wherever we find it. What is this efficacy? Are we to believe what we are told, that such things as singing and dancing actually have an effect on the world? Can the performers really mean what they say? Aren't we to find here some fault in logic, some peculiar way of communicating, some hidden meaning, some primitive deficiency? I think not. Still, to take the truth of this assertion seriously is the greatest challenge we will meet in the study of ritual, and it is absolutely essential that we face it. Finally, even if we try to take all of it seriously, we are struck by the complexity of the ritual acts, the singing and dancing, the preparations, the costumes, the time and effort, the esoteric rites. The philosopher, Suzanne Langer, has said that ritual is the language of religion, but if we accept this observation and consider that it takes all the complexity of ritual to convey such simple messages as those stated by the performers, we can only conclude that it must be a very inefficient language. There must be more to the meaning of ritual than conveying these simple messages. We must figure that out, too.

Ritual occurs on so many occasions in culture that even to construct a catalog of types and occasions would not be possible here. But that is not our interest in any case. Let it be sufficient here to note that ritual commonly accompanies the passages from state to state in the life cycle and in the annual cycles of activities; it accompanies moments of crisis; it accompanies major moments, when unions or separations take place, such as journeys, marriages, friendships; it embodies acts of transcendence and immanence, celebration and consecration.

To introduce the subject of ritual and to illustrate how we may come to terms with the problems in understanding which we have just described, we will discuss several examples selected in such a way that they represent major types of rituals commonly found in nonliterate cultures.

RITES OF PASSAGE—LIFE CYCLE

The transformative powers of ritual are especially clear in what are broadly known as rites of passage. These are rites which bring about the change from one state to another in any domain of culture. These rites may be found on such occasions as birth, initiation into adulthood, death, entrance into secret societies or offices, or at various times of the year, such as the transition from winter to summer or from one year to another.

In the classic study of these rites, Arnold van Gennep illuminated a striking feature of this kind of ritual. The structure of rites of passage is such that the transformation between two states, say from childhood to adulthood, does not occur in a simple one-step movement from the first state to the second but rather by a three-phase process. First, a phase of the ritual brings about a *separation* from the state in which one has existed, but the status which results is characterized by its ambiguity; that is, there is a period recognized in the ritual transition where those who have been separated from the state they were in exist for a time in no culturally recognized state at all. They are in the margins between recognized states. They are marginal or *liminal* peoples, existing only in the interstices of culture. This is the most significant aspect of rites of passage, and we will want to discuss this condition further. From this marginal condition the passage or transition is concluded by the rites of *reaggregation* or reincorporation, in which the persons are introduced into their new state or status.

The symbolism of the threefold structure of rites of passage is often quite clear, and we can easily see the underlying ideas. In rites of passage the initial task is to symbolically produce the death of the person, at least as he had been identified by himself and others prior to this moment. The liminal period is *sensory threshold* necessary to the experience of death; it symbolizes the status of death: One is in no state at all. Then, too, this symbolic condition of nonexistence is the appropriate precondition to being born into a new state. This ritual process is one of death and rebirth. It is irreversible and completely transforming. Let us look at an example to see more clearly how this takes place.

Initiation rites for youths are very common among nonliterate peoples and doubtless are of great antiquity. Scheduled initiation rites for groups of boys are more common than for girls, which is probably linked to the fact that in many cultures the beginning of menstruation signals the need for the initiation of girls, whereas boys have no such physiological sign of their coming of age.

The initiation scenario for the youths of the Wiradjuri in eastern Australia is fairly representative of the peoples in this area.[1] At the appointed time, a special place for initiation activities is designated in the bush away from the village. The women in the village are covered with branches and blankets when a group of men arrive whirling bull-roarers (sticks attached to the end of a string which make a roaring sound when whirled), beating the ground with sticks, and throwing burning brands. During this havoc the youths to be initiated are seized and led away into the bush. The women and other children are not allowed to look during this part of the rite, and they only hear and feel the fearful effects of these activities, which amount to a rite of separation. When all becomes quiet and the women inspect what has happened, they find their boys gone and nothing but ashes and burning sticks all about them.

The explanation given the women by the men is that Daramulun, a spirit being, has been present and that he has tried to kill them all. They say that he has eaten the boys, but that they will soon be regurgitated and revived as full-grown men. The voice of Daramulun is identified with the fearful sound made by the bull-roarers.

The treatment of space is a highly symbolic aspect of the initiation process. The two spaces designated are the village and a place "in the bush." The village is a place which denotes family and society maintained through the lineage of the women. The bush is a place of animals, a place not of human order or presence. Hence, the forceful removal of the boys symbolically brings about their death to society as they have known it, even in terms of the meanings associated with the ground on which the initiation takes place. It is significant in this respect that the Wiradjuri name for the initiation rites is *guringal,* which means "belonging to the bush." As the youths are conducted into the bush they are forced to walk with their eyes on the ground between their feet. All about them the voice of Daramulun threatens.

During the ensuing liminal phase of the initiation rite, the youths are often greatly frightened. At one point in the initiation process, they are covered with blankets and told that Daramulun is coming to eat them. With bull-roarers close by, the men reach under the blanket of each youth, and with hammer and chisel, they knock out an incisor tooth. The boys are told that the spirit is taking their teeth although sparing their lives.

---

[1] For descriptions of this ritual, see R. H. Matthews, "The Burbung of the Wiradthuri Tribes," *The Journal of the Anthropological Institute of Great Britain and Ireland,* Vol. XXV (1896), 295–317; and A. W. Howitt, *The Native Tribes of South-East Australia* (London: Macmillan, 1904), pp. 516–63.

FIGURE 6.2. Bora ritual: covered novices led by guardians down the secret-sacred ground (Australia). (From Ronald M. Berndt, *Australian Aboriginal Religion*, 1974. Courtesy of E. J. Brill.)

This liminal phase culminates in a most frightful experience for the youths. The boys are placed again under blankets and told that Daramulun is coming to burn them. Fires are built near the boys, and as they reach a crackling blaze, the sounds of the bull-roarers approach the boys in a most threatening way. But when the boys appear sufficiently terrified, their blankets are removed and they are directed to look at what is about them. They see, for the first time, the source of the voice of Daramulun. It is only their elders whirling sticks on the ends of pieces of string. When they notice this, the men say, "There he is! There is Daramulun!" Then the boys are shown how the bull-roarers are made and how they are whirled. They may even do it themselves. The boys are then sworn to secrecy and the bull-roarers are destroyed. With teeth missing and often with their bodies painted with red ochre or blood, the initiates, who are now men, return to the village. As they enter, it is clear to the women that the boys have been killed by Daramulun and have been reborn as men. They will be known by new adult names and will reside outside the homes of their parents.

From a cultural perspective, it is not difficult for us to see that initiation effects a transformation of the youths to adulthood. The women know that their boys have been violently separated from them by the spirit Daramulun, who has also wreaked havoc in their village. After this experience, they observe the boys returning, blood smeared and with tooth removed (or in some instances circumcised). They are not the same; they are now men.

We can see that the symbols of death and rebirth permeate the ritual process. The symbolic motif of being eaten and regurgitated is quite common in the symbolism of rites of passage and their associated oral traditions. From the perspective of the youths, although there must certainly be something exhilarating about being the focus of these ordeals, they experience fear and considerable discomfort. They are forced into a position which is without status, and they experience in this condition the paradox which it embodies. They are living, yet they are dead. They are human beings, yet they have no place. While they give themselves totally over to their elders and the spirits, they develop an intense sense of camaraderie as fellow initiates, a relationship which will continue throughout their adulthood.

Although it is not difficult to see how the initiation rites function to bring about a transformation from one level of the social structure to another, difficulties arise when we try to consider it as a religious initiation; but it is that as well. It is through the initiation rites that the boys are introduced to the knowledge of the spiritual and ritual domain of culture. Through the transformative powers of the initiation rites they enter their formal religious life. But when we review this aspect of the rites we are struck by the obvious chicanery of the men who conduct them, although it must be noted that it is not a necessary feature of all initiation rites. However, it cannot be overlooked that these men are quite consciously and purposefully setting up tricks to frighten the boys. Most shocking is the manner in which Daramulun is revealed. During the rite the youths are told time after time to identify the presence of Daramulun with the roaring sound. But in the end, they are shown that this sound is nothing but the noise of a stick when whirled about on a string, a thing which they can easily make.

We are back to the question of truth, and we cannot be relieved of dealing with it by dismissing this as a degenerated rite or some aberrance, for we can observe this same element of directed trickery in the initiation rites of many nonliterate peoples. Indeed, we can even find that in many cultures the initiates are profoundly shocked or disappointed by such a revelation. How can we account for the religious significance of this kind of act, which at its surface seems to say, if anything, that the religion to which one enters is either a sham or a cruel joke.

In attempting to deal with this factor we must appreciate the fact that the necessary feature of any religious initiation is to produce a transformation from seeing what is concretely before one's eyes to being able to see at the level of reality which is not so obvious because it is spiritual in character. From the perspective of religion, the initiation process must deal a death blow to satisfaction from seeing the world as simply what it appears to be in its physical form, and it must give birth to a life in which the spiritual and sacred character of reality may be accepted and appreciated.

In the Wiradjuri initiation process we can see that much of its intent is to emphasize the very way of viewing reality that must be overcome. The men take numerous steps to assure that the boys identify the presence of the spirit Daramulun with audible sounds and felt actions. It seems quite clear that this identity is constructed only so that it can be exploded. The trick is intentional. In the climactic moment of the liminal portion of the rite, the youths *see* that what had appeared to be so fearful and threatening was only a stick on a string. What is accomplished in this process is a disenchantment with a naive view of reality, that is, with the view that things are what they appear to be. The trickery serves to disenchant the initiate with this view, and the experience of disenchantment can never be reversed. You can only be fooled once in such a way. Once the truth is revealed, the naive view is dead. Thus, being forced to abandon one's ingrained notion of reality, one experiences a true death of the former self, in this case the status and perceptions of youth. And this loss of self constitutes the concrete transformation signified by the symbolic dying experience in the rites of initiation.[2]

The birth into adulthood and into the religious life is not one in which there is fullness of knowledge. If anything there is only confusion or the opening to knowledge which may be acquired through a lifetime of experience. The effect of the disenchantment is to bring the initiate to the threshold of revelation upon having fully experienced the death of the old self.

RITES OF PASSAGE—ANNUAL CYCLE

Just as there are distinct states through which one must pass in the cycle of life, there are states or periods which must be traversed in living through a cycle of time. The most common time base is a year, and the most prominent rite of passage is the new year's rite. The symbolism of death and rebirth of time is borne in Western cultures in the familiar scythe-carrying white-haired and aged father time and the unclad innocent baby new year. In nonliterate cultures there is an immense variety of these rites of passage and they are often very complex. Reluctantly, I forgo the description of several of these rites for a fuller presentation of one example.

The example, however, is satisfying for it permits us to discuss many aspects of the new year's ritual process. We will look at a people in Indonesia called the Ngaju Dayak who live in south Borneo. The Ngaju Dayak are composed of many tribes who name themselves in correspondence with the rivers on which they reside. The example comes from the important study of Ngaju

---

[2] For a discussion of this aspect of initiation, see Sam Gill, "Disenchantment," *Parabola*, Vol. I, No. 3 (1976), 6–13.

religion by Hans Schärer, a work which is an outstanding example of a cultural approach to the study of the religion of a nonliterate people.[3]

The Ngaju Dayak spend a great amount of their time preparing, planting, and tending rice fields cut into the forest around their villages. Beginning in May the men of the village start looking for places in the forest where they can make their fields. When the fields are marked out, the family clears the area. After the bush and undergrowth are chopped out the large trees are felled and left to dry in the fields. During late August and September the dried brush is burned in the fields, providing ash to fertilize the soil. The rice is planted in late September and early October, and the plants are tended until the harvest is reaped in February and March. The sustenance activities totally engage the entire community from May through March. With the harvest complete, the people return to the village for two or three months before it is time to begin preparing the fields again. It is during this time, while the people are away from the fields, that the new year's feast is held. Many activities characterize this period of time: sporting events, fishing and hunting expeditions, feasting, and ritual performances. It is a joyful time, yet to the outsider it may appear to be a time of disorder and saturnalia. No social or moral rule seems to reign. Mass sexual intercourse occurs, ownership or property rights are ignored, and it is the time of major sacrifices. Against our own experiences we should not be too surprised at what appears to be disorder and chaos on the eve of the new year, but we must paint in more of the background to appreciate what is happening in this situation.

In Schärer's study of this culture, he shows that all of Ngaju life is a manifestation or reflection of their conception of god. We can see the character of this conception most immediately in the story of the creation of the Ngaju cosmos.

In the beginning there was only formless water, but out of the water rose two mountains, Gold Mountain and Jewel Mountain, which were the seats of two supreme deities. These mountains clashed together repeatedly, and each time something was created: the sun and moon, the vault of heaven, the clouds, and the various features of the earth.

Then Mahatala, the supreme deity of the Gold Mountain who reigns in the Upperworld, appeared and stretched out his hand so that drops of water fell from his fingers. From these drops the divine maiden, Jata, ruling in the Underworld, emerged from the primal waters. From her earring she made the earth. Together they created the rivers and the first human beings. Mahatala, after conferring with Jata, raised his headdress and it became the Tree of Life. From its golden leaves and ivory fruit Mahatala's sister made a rice tree, which later would be the source of rice. This sister also possessed a female hornbill in a

---

[3] Hans Schärer, *Ngaju Religion: The Conception of God Among a South Borneo People* (The Hague: Martinus Nijhoff, 1963).

golden cage which she freed. The bird flew to the Tree of Life, alighted on it, and fed on its buds and fruit. Mahatala transformed his jewel-studded golden dagger into a male hornbill which also flew to the Tree of Life. Envious of the better food the female hornbill seemed to be getting, the male hornbill attacked her and a terrible fight ensued, which caused the destruction of the Tree of Life. As the tree was being destroyed, the blossoms and fruit were transformed into a golden boat and from the knotty excrescences of the tree came a maiden. She entered the boat and set forth on the primal waters. From the stump of the tree came a boat made of jewel, and from the slashed throat of the female hornbill came a youth who entered the jewel boat and set out on the primal waters.

Eventually the two boats ran together and the youth fell in love with the maiden, but she would not agree to marry him until he had found a place for them to live. Mahatala made for them an island on the back of a watersnake, but the maiden still would not marry the youth because she had no house. Jata emerged from the waters to build them a house in which to live, and in their marriage, the youth and maiden became the ancestors and culture heroes of the Ngaju Dayak. It is in the stories of these figures that the Ngaju find the model for their entire way of life.

This story bears much of the Ngaju conception of god, a conception intricately bound in the interrelationship between duality and unity, between the forces of destruction and creation. From the undifferentiated primal waters came two aspects of god, represented in the two mountains and the two supreme deities. The one is associated with the underworld, with destruction and the watersnake; the other, with the upperworld, with creation and the hornbill. When they came together their union produced life in the cosmos, symbolized by the Tree of Life. But the creation of culture and the Ngaju way of life came about only as a result of the destruction of the Tree of Life by the ferocious fight of the male and female hornbills. Schärer identifies this complex interrelationship as reflecting the ambivalence of god in the Ngaju conception.

Let us turn now to the interrelationship between this concept of god, the story of creation, and the description we have made of the events of the annual cycle of life, especially the events during the period between the harvest and the preparation of new fields. Based on the Ngaju view, we cannot make any meaningful distinction between secular and sacred times of the year, for the work in the fields, as well as the festivals in the villages, is done according to the divine models established in primal time. In the mundane work of designating, clearing, and preparing the fields for planting, and the work of planting, tending, protecting, and harvesting the rice, the Ngaju Dayak enact the divinely given order of the world. The same duality which characterizes the cosmic order is reflected, for example, in the division of labor between men and women and in the distinction between fields and forest. But the duality is interdependent, and in this relationship is achieved the unity which creates both community and the means to sustain that community. The Ngaju consider this period of life-sustaining labor to be a year, the period of time set forth by the divine ancestors for the orderly way of life. It is modeled upon the events in the primal era as established by the divine forebearers of culture.

It is in light of these Ngaju conceptions that we must now look at the period following the harvest. Notably the Ngaju refer to this as *helat nyelo,* or "the time between the years." It is a time outside of time. In the Ngaju view, a year is equal to a whole era in the existence of the world. This year having elapsed, the creation has run its course and the people must return to the Tree of Life and accede to the primal conditions, so that life may again be regenerated or recreated. In the events of this "time between the years" we can observe the symbolization and reactualization of the events which took place in the primal era and which caused the creation of the Ngaju cosmos and life.

During this time between the years, the major divisions of society, which are also identified with the hornbill and the watersnake, come together in the village. A staff, representing Mahatala and maleness, to which is attached a cloth banner, representing Jata and femaleness, is erected at the village center. The erection of this standard is one of the most important ritual acts, for it is symbolic of the Tree of Life. The absence of social differentiation and the presence of mass sexual intercourse symbolize the undifferentiated state of unity out of which cosmic creation took place. The emphasis during this timeless time is on the totality that is a unity, in contrast to the unity of an interdependent duality that characterizes the dynamics of order, which prevails throughout the Ngaju year and the created cosmos. Although it may appear to be chaos or disorder, from the perspective of the Ngaju conception of god and creation, this disorder can be recognized as another kind of order. It is a reacquisition of the cosmic unity and wholeness which characterized primal time. One can observe that the Tree of Life, in which the duality is dissolved, encompasses the entire people; they all live in the Tree of Life during the "time between the years."

The conclusion of the new year's rite follows the pattern of the creation scenario, with the events of human and animal sacrifice and the destruction of the emblems which symbolize the Tree of Life. In this destruction the primal unity gives way to the creation of a new year, with renewed social order, new fields, new crops, all proceeding according to the divinely destined way of life.

It is notable that this rite of passage retains the structure previously discussed—separation, liminality, and reaggregation. Death and rebirth are not only present, they are also incorporated into the very conceptions of god and cosmic creativity. From the undifferentiated formless unity arises duality, symbolized by the mountains, the male and female deities, and the upper and lower worlds. In the comingling or unity of this duality arises the potential for life, itself a kind of unity symbolized by the Tree of Life. But this Tree of Life cannot give forth life except in its destruction, its sacrifice, its division. The new year's rites bear the Ngaju conceptions of the interdependence of death and life, destruction and creation, unity and diversity, and human time and primal timelessness.

In the Ngaju system of thought, mediation between aspects of the duality is especially important and can be seen in many areas of Ngaju religion. The priestly group, for example, whose official role is that of mediation, are chosen and serve by their suitability for this task. The priests (*basir*) are hermaphrodites, thus bearing in their sexuality their ability to both distinguish and encompass the primal duality. The priests engage in homosexual acts, as reflected in the term *basir*, which means barren or unfruitful. Their female counterparts, the *balian*, are chosen from the slaves, who are ordinarily considered unclean. They serve as priestly prostitutes. Sexual intercourse with a *balian* is a sacred act which transports men from the present to the primal era. It places them in the Tree of Life at one with god.

It is notable that mediators are chosen from those outside of recognized social and sexual positions. The priestly group mediates between social groups, but they also belong to the entire community. By standing at once between the Upperworld and the Underworld and actually being identified with these worlds together, the priestly group embodies the character of the ambivalent godhead. To have union with a priestly figure is to enter into the sacred reality of god.

Acts of sacrifice also are significant in terms of mediating between human and divine realms, as we will discuss in the next section.

One other aspect of Schärer's understanding of Ngaju religion seems relevant here for it bears on the potency of ritual. Schärer found that the whole of Ngaju Dayak life proceeded in accordance with their conception of the ambivalence of god; yet he found that their conception of god was modeled upon their own understanding of the nature of human existence. He says that "man has elevated himself into the transcendental world and has deified himself, i.e., he has removed the community, its laws, tribal area, life and thought into an absolute and sacred sphere where it is objectified. The world and society have not emanated from the deities, but the deities and their world are the human world and society pronounced sacred by man himself."[4] This statement does not mean that Ngaju religion, Ngaju reality, is but a figment in a fanciful mind. Rather it assures us of the reality of Ngaju religion. It helps us to appreciate the significance of the efficacy of Ngaju ritual acts, for they are keys to the process by which the Ngajus elevate themselves into that sphere where they can enact cosmic creations, the sphere where ordinary human limitations are transcended. Through ritual demarking the annual cycles, they are one with the gods and heroic ancestors.

SACRIFICIAL RITUALS

The Ainu, a people living in northern Japan who probably came from Siberia, capture a bear cub and raise it to maturity. It becomes the subject of a sacrificial festival called *Kamui Omante,* which means "to send off the god." When the time

---

4 *Ibid.,* p. 157.

FIGURE 6.3. Bear sacrifice. (Hand scroll [Makimono]. Ink and paint on paper, Ainu, Japan, circa. 1840. 26 1/2 x 491 cm. Courtesy of the Brooklyn Museum.)

comes, the bear is bound so that its struggles serve only to choke it. The people taunt it into a state of rage and shoot it again and again with blunt arrows. After it is exhausted, the killing wound is finally given and all the people rush to squeeze the life out of it as it is dying. The bear carcass becomes the food of the feast.[5]

In Africa the cattle of Nuer and Dinka herdsmen are commonly sacrificed. All sorts of maladies, pending dangers, legal and moral infringements, and events for celebration are occasions for sacrifice. The sacrifice is made to protect the sacrificer and his kin by sending the malevolent spirits away or by endowing the occasion with a benevolent spiritual presence. In either case, an ox is tethered to a post while the sacrificer, ritually gesturing with his spear which is held in his right hand, makes a long speech during which he indicates the purpose and concern of the sacrifice. The animal is then killed and immediately butchered. Its meat is distributed among the community according to carefully defined rules related to the purpose of the sacrifice and one's kinship to the sacrificer.[6]

---

[5] Joseph M. Kitagawa, "Ainu Bear Festival (Iyomante)," *History of Religions,* Vol. 1, No. 1 (1961), 95–151.

[6] For a discussion and description of these sacrificial acts, see E. E. Evans-Pritchard, *Nuer Religion* (New York: Oxford University Press, 1956); and Godfrey Lienhardt, *Divinity and Experience: The Religion of the Dinka* (London: Oxford University Press, 1961).

In the Sun Dances of the northern plains cultures in North America, individuals make sacrifices for the benefit of the whole people in the form of self-immolation—the cutting of pieces from one's flesh; the piercing of the flesh to permit tethering to sacred objects; the dehydration and exhaustion of fasting, dancing, and staring at the sun.[7]

Many more examples could be named, but these are sufficient to introduce us to the events of ritual sacrifice, which are common among nonliterate peoples. Our difficulty comes in attempting to understand them as meaningful religious acts. We must ask how the purposeful infliction of suffering and death upon animals, even human beings, can be appreciated and seen as justifiable to the people in any religious tradition. To date, the most broadly accepted theory of sacrifice stems from the statements of E. B. Tylor, one of the nineteenth century fathers of anthropology. He suggested that sacrifice was a kind of gift to the gods for purposes of self-denial or homage.[8] From this point of view, the sacrificial victim served as a gift to mediate between human beings and the gods. This view has been developed and restated in many forms, but it still is the most common basis for understanding sacrifice. It seems to fit some aspects of sacrificial rites, for they usually involve something given—a bear, an ox, a piece of flesh—with the expectation of some reward—good health, good crops, a new status in life. But even in view of these brief sacrificial scenarios, the language and ideological framework of the gift theory seems to be aimed at aspects of sacrifice other than the religious.[9]

We can benefit from the insight of a recent study of sacrifice by Richard Hecht, who was especially concerned with its religious significance. He tells us that in the performance of sacrificial rituals, the shape and meaning of reality are communicated to and formed for the people. In other words, from the point of view of the people performing the rituals, the world is dependent upon the performance of the sacrificial act in that it imposes form on the phenomena of the world. This view casts quite a different light upon our understanding of sacrifice, for now we must see that it is a human responsibility to perform sacrificial acts in order to maintain the order of one's world and the meaning in one's way of life.[10]

We can take advantage of the discussion of the new year's ritual of the Ngaju Dayak for a more careful discussion of an example of sacrifice from this suggested perspective, for the Ngaju Dayak practiced, until recently, both headhunting and human sacrifice. The principal occasions for sacrifice are male

---

[7] For a recent survey of the Sun Dance in various Native American cultures, see Joseph G. Jorgensen, *The Sun Dance Religion* (Chicago: University of Chicago Press, 1972).

[8] For his discussion of sacrifice, see Edward B. Tylor, *Primitive Culture* (London: John Murray, 1873), Vol. II, pp. 375–410.

[9] For a thorough critical review of the gift theory of sacrifice, see Richard D. Hecht, *Sacrifice, Comparative Study and Interpretation,* Ph.D. Dissertation, University of California, Los Angeles, 1976, pp. 92–105.

[10] For the full discussion of this new direction in the interpretation of sacrifice as a religious act, see *ibid.,* pp. 205–17.

initiation rites, marriage ceremonies, deaths, and most especially the culmination of the new year's rite as described above. Let us look at that ritual of sacrifice.

You will recall that the new year's rite, taking place in "the time between the years" (*helat nyelo*), is a reenactment of the sacred events which gave birth to the cosmos as told in the Ngaju Dayak stories. The banner representing the fruit-laden Tree of Life is erected in the center of the village, and from its destruction, the story tells us, comes the creation of life and cosmic order. This event is reenacted as we previously described. The major sacrifice of the year takes place as part of the reenactment of the destruction of the Tree of Life. A slave is sacrificed to reenact symbolically the fight of the hornbills who destroyed the Tree of Life and met their deaths in the process. Beginning about sunset on the last day of the interyear period, a slave is tied to a sacrificial post in the village center. All the people come to this place and dance around him, stabbing him with spears, daggers, swords, and blowpipes. In this way the entire community participates in the ritual battle and in the infliction of death upon the victim. This event continues throughout the night and concludes when the deathblow is finally given to the slave about sunrise. Over the body of the slave, the priest pronounces that all illness and pain, all affliction and fever, have been lifted from the people. The whole community participates in the burial of the slave, who is placed face down in a grave outside the village limits, which is symbolically outside of the orderly world. Each person stamps dirt on the grave and is marked with the blood of the victim in a manner which symbolizes the cardinal directions of the orderly cosmos.[11]

In greeting the sun of this new day, the people also greet a new year and a newly created cosmos. The Tree of Life has been annihilated, the hornbills have killed each other, and the creation of the world has taken place. In this new time and new world they proceed to the tasks of their fields once again.

We can see in the events of the sacrificial ritual that much more is taking place than an exchange of gifts. Human communities are participating in the very processes of creation by exercising the formula that death and life are intimately and profoundly interrelated and interdependent.

If we are inclined to be shocked and even offended by what appear to be acts of cruelty or bizarre savagery, as observers of the sacrificial rites of nonliterate peoples have commonly been, we must remember that sacrifice is at the very core of many of the religious traditions of the great civilizations. Lame Deer, an Oglala, responded to this familiar reaction of white Americans to the piercing of flesh in the Sun Dance by saying, "The idea of enduring pain so that others may live should not strike you as strange. Do you not in your churches pray to one who is 'pierced,' nailed to a cross for the sake of his people? No In-

---

[11] Schärer, *Ngaju Religion*, pp. 139–41.

dian ever called a white man uncivilized for his beliefs or forbade him to worship as he pleased.''[12]

It is also important to note that it is the enacting of the sacrificial rites more than the actual rendering of a human or animal death that brings about the cosmic order. For example, if the Nuer do not have a suitable animal available when the occasion for sacrifice arises, they may substitute for the ox a nonedible cucumber. In every respect the sacrifice is carried out as if there were an ox being sacrificed, even to the point of calling the cucumber ''ox.'' In recent years, the Ngaju Dayak have used small animals in place of slaves. This is not necessarily a sign of the degradation of sacrificial ritual but rather evidence that these people understand the efficacy of their ritual acts. Since it is the ritual acts which bring meaning and order to the world, it does not matter, when circumstantially necessary, that a cucumber is sacrificed in place of an ox.

SHAMANS

The *yurt* (tent) of a Yakat family offers protection from the Siberian tundra, which seems to stretch forever in all directions. There is special activity focused on this *yurt* as a number of people from this small community of reindeer hunters gather for the performance of a shaman. They squeeze into the *yurt* in the evening as the shaman is about to perform. The master of the house has prepared two nooses of strong leather which are secured to the shaman's shoulders and held by the people to protect him from being carried off by the spirits he is about to invoke.

As all take their places, the shaman begins to stare into the fire. When all becomes quiet the shaman yawns and begins to hiccup spasmodically. Now and again he is shaken by nervous tremors. He dons his shamanic costume, adorned with perhaps forty pounds of metal ornaments, and begins to smoke. Soon his face grows pale and then his head falls on his breast. His eyes are nearly closed. The hide of a white mare is spread in the center of the *yurt;* the shaman takes a drink of cold water and turns in each of the cardinal directions, spitting water to the right and left. An assistant throws horsehair on the fire, and as he covers the fire with ashes, the darkness in the *yurt* grows, as does the intense silence of anticipation.

> Suddenly a succession of shrill cries, piercing as the screech of steel, sounds from no one knows where; then all is silent again. Another cry; and now from above, now from below, now before, now behind the shaman rise mysterious sounds: nervous, terrifying yawns, hysterical hiccups; it is as if one heard the plaintive cry of the lapwing mingled with the crowing of a falcon and interrupted

---

[12] John (Fire) Lame Deer and Richard Erdoes, *Lame Deer Seeker of Visions* (New York: Simon & Schuster, 1972), p. 208.

by the whistling of the woodcock; it is the shaman making these sounds by changing the tone of his voice.[13]

Silence reigns again for a surprising moment. The shaman soon takes up his drum and begins to sing. Soft at first, the drumming and singing slowly rise in volume until the shaman is bellowing. Again the cries of eagles, the lamenting of lapwings, the songs of woodcocks and cuckoos are heard. But the singing grows even louder, then stops abruptly. Again the surprise of silence.

Again and again this sequence is repeated as the shaman builds the intensity and enters the ecstatic state in which he can invoke his helping spirits. The spirits finally arrive, knocking the shaman to the floor. But upon being revived by the banging of strong iron over him, he begins leaping violently about the *yurt,* animated by his spirit helpers.

The fire is rekindled, and while drumming, the shaman leaps about crying wildly, pausing in his dance to sing the songs of his shamanic powers. Thus prepared, the shaman approaches the person whose illness is the reason for the performance, and he begins to summon the cause of the illness in order to cast it out. With much animation the shaman, with the help of his spirits, finds the malady in the person's body, and laying hold of it, takes it to the center of the room and dramatizes the departure of the malady by kicking it, spitting it away, and driving it off with his hands and breath.[14]

Although the word *shaman* derives from the Tungusic (Siberian) word *šaman,* and is often used in a narrow sense to describe a very specific religious phenomenon of this area, it has come to be used in a much broader sense to refer to any individual who holds the power and knowledge to willfully utilize ecstatic techniques in order to perform for his or her community services which require intervention into the spiritual realm. Shamanism refers to the practices of such persons and does not refer to a religion or type of religion as such, for shamanism always occurs in the context of a religious tradition rather than itself constituting one.

Again we are faced with problems of understanding these ritual performances. When told that the Yakat shaman whose performance we have just described cured the illness of the person he was performing for, we are faced again with the question of truth. Are we to believe what we are told without having to dismiss what we know of modern scientific medical practices? Can we understand and appreciate enough of the religious world view of these peoples to understand what they mean by health and how they understand life and how they see that this shamanic performance operates within this view in a way which is efficacious? Let us turn to a discussion of the world view in which shamanism ordinarily occurs.

———
[13] Wenceslas Sieroszewski, "Du chamanisme d'apres les croyances des Yakoutes," *Revue de l'histoire des religions,* Vol. XLVI (1902), 326; as quoted in Mircea Eliade, *Shamanism: Archaic Techniques of Ecstasy* (Princeton, N.J.: Princeton University Press, 1964), p. 230.

[14] Eliade, *Shamanism,* pp. 229–32.

FIGURE 6.4. Tungus shaman. (From Charles H. Hawes, *In the Uppermost East.* Reprinted by Arno Press, 1971.)

Basic to the world view of cultures in which shamans perform is that the cosmos is formed in multiple layers. There are commonly three, with the earth situated between upper and lower worlds inhabited by spirits and deities. There is a belief that some of these spirits have the power to affect the lives of human beings. This belief is especially clear in the theories of disease. Illness is attributed to the loss of the soul or vitality either by theft or by the enticement of offended spirits or deities. It may also be caused by the projection of harmful objects or substances into the body by entities from these other worlds. The shaman has power to intercede in such matters because of his alliance with certain helping spirits whom he is able to call. In the shaman's performance he becomes allied with these spirits, and together they engage in the process of discerning the situation which is causing the illness and then rectifying the problem.

The shaman's duties often require that he make a magical flight to the spirit world. For example, when performing as a clairvoyant, psychopomp (escort of the soul of the deceased to the domain of the dead), or deliverer of a sacrificial offering to the spiritual world, the shaman makes such a flight either to the upper world(s) or lower world(s). The rituals and ritual symbolism of shamanism permit the dramatization of this magical flight for the community. A tree may be erected in the center of the ritual domain, representing the world axis or pillar, the channel of communication among the various levels of the cosmos. In a state of ecstasy, imitating the voices of his helping spirits, commonly identified with animals and birds, the shaman ascends the tree branch by branch, enacting the journey through cosmic levels. Stopping at each branch he describes through the voices of his spirit helpers what is happening.

Looking back at the Yakat shamanic cure, we can see that the ill health for which it was performed was not seen simply as a physiological or psychological matter confined to the mind and body of the person suffering. It was seen as a cosmic affair. It was caused by some spiritual intervention in human affairs which left the person with his or her vitality impaired by an object of malevolence or obstruction. The performance of the shaman intervenes in this situation and is effective because he has the power to call upon his helping spirits and thereby to break the plane of ordinary experience in order to diagnose the problem and to rectify it. The performance of the shaman assures the presence of the spirits, for their voices are heard, and he enacts the dispersal of the life-threatening matter.

As in our discussion of sacrifice, we can see that the ritual acts of the shaman must be understood as the human performance of those acts which give meaning and order to the world. The shaman is a specialist in such matters, adept at making repairs to imbalances and disorders.

CLOWNS

We began this chapter with a description of the stately occasion of the Hopi ceremonial Niman, the annual farewell dance of the kachinas. I would like to return to the Hopi to consider another aspect of ritual, the performances of clowns. During the kachina season at Hopi, clowns play perhaps as important a role in most ceremonials as do the kachinas. The clowns' hilarious activities, played out during the two days of the public performance, seem often to defy any organization, so disorderly and unpredictable are their character. But despite this appearance, over the course of the performance clowning proceeds according to a clear and well-defined ritual scenario. It is the way of clowning not only to assure the clowns freedom to challenge the orderly and accepted but also to assure that the tensions and challenges they bring will be resolved.

The kachinas make their first appearance in the village at sunrise on the days of public performance. Throughout the day of kachina dancing in the plaza, they epitomize order and perfection. The clowns' arrival is unexpected, a surprise which creates a disturbance, a distraction. Often they do not appear until noon. While the kachinas are dancing in the plaza, one hears a loud call from the tops of the houses on the west side of the plaza: *"Yaahahay!"* As the people turn to see what is happening, the clowns drop down out of sight. But immediately they pop up again, raising their arms as they call. Four times they give this call, which proclaims that they have reached the paradise foretold to the Hopi when they first entered this world. But their entrance into that promised domain is surprising, as they slide down ropes upside down and get caught on ladders. Comically they stumble and fall into the plaza where the kachinas are performing.

Once in the plaza, they see the food and green plants which the kachinas have brought, and they exclaim how glorious a place they have found. Hearing the kachinas' songs they begin to grope about for these spirit beings whom they pretend they cannot see. Eventually one of the clowns bumps into a kachina and claims him as his possession. The other clowns immediately attempt to proclaim their rights to the kachinas by trying to surround as many as possible.

When the kachinas retire to their resting place between dances, the clowns perform a wide variety of skits satirizing many aspects of Hopi life. One of the most common is focused on building a house. Upon surveying the plaza, the clowns decide to take up residence in this paradise, and they set out to build a house. The head clown directs the activities and sends the other clowns off in all directions to procure the building materials needed. He orders logs from the San Francisco peaks. The clowns reenter the plaza with logs, but these are rejected by the head clown who says, "I sent you for logs; these are only ashes!" And he sends them off again. This time the clowns bring back ashes, which greatly pleases the head clown for he admires them as fine logs. Taking the ashes he strews them on the ground outlining a house. While he does this, he satirically imitates the traditional Hopi songs of housebuilding. Clowns commonly carry rag dolls in their belts, and when the house is complete, the head clown will take his doll and set it in the house with his blankets. He instructs the doll as he would a wife to prepare food for him and to be hospitable to his guests.

During kachina dances, great quantities of food are brought into the plaza for distribution by the kachinas and clowns among the people of the village. One of the chief characteristics of clowns is gluttony. They eat constantly throughout the day, consuming whole pies, watermelons, and amazing quantities of food. Their humor often centers on sexuality, which is another of their strengths, and skits often include one or more clowns who dress like women with sexual features often exaggerated.

Upon describing clown activities Emory Sekaquaptewa, a Hopi, explained that the key to the practice of Hopi clowning is to understand that all people are clowns. Given the promise of a future paradise as the destiny of the Hopi way, it is the plight of the Hopi to be subject to their own humanity—their biological needs for food, shelter, sex, and the faults of greed, selfishness, and foolishness. The clowns in their actions and the skits enact the story of humanity. In these

FIGURE 6.5. "The Delight-Makers." (A painting of Hopi clowns by Fred Kabotie. Courtesy of Museum of the American Indian, Heye Foundation, N.Y.)

humorous presentations, especially in contrast with the kachina performances, the people can reflect on their nature and learn of the difficulties, but promises, of their way of life.[15]

There is a gradual development in this scenario of Hopi clowning. The clowns are reminded of their foolishness from time to time by Owl Kachina, who appears first at the corners of the plaza and throws pebbles at the clowns. The pebbles are to serve the clowns as pangs of conscience. As expected, they ignore these as minor irritants. But each time when Owl returns he is more threatening; eventually he is accompanied by fearful-looking warrior kachinas brandishing yucca whips. By the fourth appearance there is such a show of force by Owl's group that it is clear that the clowns will meet their end. Rushing into the plaza, the warrior kachinas soundly whip the clowns for their wrongful actions. After the whipping they are greeted by the kachinas with handshakes and sprinkled with water as a sign of purification. Still clowns are always clowns, and their antics continue even as they appear one by one before the assembled kachinas to enact, with great humor and wit, the confession of their wrong ways.

Clowns, fools, and contraries are common in the religious traditions of nonliterate peoples and are found throughout North America, Africa, and Oceania. The most common scholarly explanation focuses on their function as entertainers. Seen in this way their role has been dismissed as comic relief to the seriousness and formality of religious ritual, in that it has been supposed that such tedious ritual seriousness could not be endured without some comic relief. This theory is perhaps not incorrect, but the effect is to distract us from

---

[15] For a Hopi presentation of clowning, see Emory Sekaquaptewa, "One More Smile for a Hopi Clown," *Parabola*, Vol. IV, No. 1 (1979), 6–9.

understanding the full religious importance of clowns. The prayer of the Hopi clown, uttered as he is about to perform, is "May I gain at least one smile." And the extent to which the Hopi clowns make the people laugh is the measure of their performance. But the religious significance of humorous entertainment in a ritual context may be as great as any other part of the ritual. It takes both the kachinas and the clowns to present and enact the Hopi way of life. In the kachinas one sees the order and perfection of the spiritual world with which the Hopi must interact throughout their lives and upon which their lives depend. It is this spiritual world to which all Hopi life is destined. But the clowns teach the Hopi the hard lessons about how human nature makes the interrelationships with this spiritual world difficult and uncertain. They teach people about their foolishness and creatureliness. Clowns behave in unsanctioned ways; they violate taboos; they pollute themselves; they act *kahopi,* that is, non-Hopi. But the effect is a strongly positive one. Not only are these matters exposed and presented publicly, which serves to defuse the tensions created by ignoring or avoiding such things, but also the actions are discouraged in the very process which exposes them. By observing the folly of the clowns and the price they finally pay, adherence to sanctioned actions is firmly established while unsanctioned actions are discouraged.

There are other dimensions to this religious phenomenon. Clowns and contraries often engage in actions that extend beyond ribaldry. Classic accounts of such actions were recorded by observers of clowns at Zuni Pueblo in New Mexico in the late nineteenth century. In these accounts we learn of clowns who attempted to outdo one another in consuming such things as urine, excrement, splinters of wood, heads of live mice, and rags. They engaged in such acts as tearing apart and devouring live dogs and encountering every sort of item considered unclean. This sort of action, far surpassing the laughable and slightly embarrassing antics of clowning, repels us and doubtless also the people before whom it is performed. It brings the clown to the point of portraying the vile and inhuman, to becoming the very personification of pollution and dirt.

When confronted with this aspect of ritual clowns we can begin to better understand their religious role. The character and significance of ritual clowning become clear when we see it as a performance balanced between acts that evoke humor and those that evoke fear. When watching any good clown performance, we can see this balance carefully maintained. As clowns begin their antics, the suggestion of violating the order of things begins to evoke a response of laughter. For example, in the backward speech common to clowns, there is a sense of play in the reversal of the world in language. Clowns say they are not thirsty when they desire a drink. The further they push this threat to order the funnier their antics seem to be. But there are limits. When clowns surpass these limits, the laughter turns to a fearful shudder. A clown threatening to tear the clothes off someone across the plaza is very funny, but when one is the object, the clown's antics are frightening and threatening. Tearing apart clothing or consuming whole pies is humorous, but tearing apart live animals and consuming excrement evoke fear and shock. Clowns often display their power by performing extraordinary feats, such as handling burning coals or plunging their hands into boiling water without being burned. These actions are at once symbolic inversions and demonstrations of the power they gain by enacting such inversions.

The clown, through a mastery of symbolic inversions, embodies an ambiguity mysterious in its quality. From this ambiguity the clown gains the kind of power which transcends the ordinary. It is the power to deal in matters of pollution and taboo. As a consequence ritual clowns commonly have the powers to heal, to bring luck in hunting and war, and to assure fertility in plants, animals, and human beings.

In clowning we see a counterpart to the role of the shaman. The clown makes no magical flights, commands no spirit helpers, enters no mystical trance, as does the shaman; yet his powers may be comparable. Indeed, it is often the role of the clown to mock with parody the shaman and the priest. In contrast, the clown gains power over pollution and disorder by becoming so closely associated with it that he is its very personification. In this we can see that the roles of the shaman, the priest, and the clown are all akin.

CONCLUSION

There are many more types of ritual that are important and commonly found in the religions of nonliterate peoples. It has not been our intention to catalog these but rather to consider the general character of ritual and to examine our difficulties in trying to appreciate and understand ritual. In all the examples we have considered, we found that ritual involves formal actions performed by members of a community so that human beings may enter into the cosmic processes of defining, creating, and shaping their world. We find something of the same tension in ritual that we did in oral traditions between the maintenance of tradition-sanctioned forms of ritual behavior and the performance of acts which are creative in the most primary sense of the word, that is, in creating the world of human meaning and thereby making the world significant.

It would be difficult to make a rigid distinction between oral traditions and ritual acts, for they are overlapping categories. Certain oral traditions, especially such forms as prayer and incantations, are also ritual acts, and many ritual acts involve aspects of oral tradition, such as songs, stories, and prayers. I do not think this distinction is of great importance since, as I have tried to demonstrate, we cannot appreciate any religious cultural acts without some familiarity with the world view and metaphysical assumptions of the people who perform them. This task is made difficult because our principal, and often only, source for this perspective is in the oral traditions and rituals.

At the outset of this chapter we raised the critical problem of considering the truth of the ritual acts of nonliterate peoples. We have wanted to avoid bracketing our understanding of their ritual acts with "as if" kinds of qualifications which would, in effect, dismiss the possible truth of the ritual acts and relegate their importance to the level of curiosity about mistaken and false beliefs. From the examples we have discussed, we must see that ritual is one of the acts in which the very criteria for truth are created, for in ritual the principles and parameters of reality are drawn and made significant.

That the truths of one culture are not the same as another is not cause for alarm, nor should it engage us in relative valuation. Rather we should focus upon the enormous capacity of human beings to make creative and meaningful responses to the profundity of life through their formal ritual actions.

7

confronting and affirming modernity

In the 1950s when anthropologist Kenelm Burridge was doing research in New Guinea, he found that several incidents had taken place among the Tangu people shortly before he had arrived. In the village of Pariakenam in a dream a youth had been given instructions for the people to follow. In his dream it was revealed that if the people performed specified rituals they would be rewarded by receiving the kind of goods that had been introduced by Europeans: tinned meat, cloth, knives, axes, beads, soap, and razor blades. Some, but not all, of the people had performed the prescribed communal feast followed by a type of trance dance in which the people formed a circle around an individual and danced and chanted rythmically, going faster and faster until the individual in the center would fall on the ground entranced. This person was then expected to speak a revelation to the people. Another individual would then take his place in the center, and the dancing would begin again.

Almost simultaneously in the neighboring village of Jumpitzir, a man dreamed of another series of rites which, if performed, promised similar rewards. In this situation men and women began by washing themselves. They assembled at the cemetery and on signal they removed their clothing and began to copulate with one another. It was a form of *coitus interruptus,* permitting the collection of the sexual fluids from both men and women. These fluids were mixed with water and poured over the burial place.[1]

---

[1] Kenelm Burridge, *Mambu: A Study of Melanesian Cargo Movements and Their Social and Ideological Background* (New York: Harper & Row, Publishers, Inc., 1960), pp. 2-3.

Were these activities unique to these people or to some rare peculiarity of their situation, they would not merit our consideration, but in fact they are far from being rare or peculiar. Such acts, often part of popular religious movements, are common among peoples, literate and nonliterate, the world over. In the most general sense, cults of this kind are referred to as "crisis cults," since their reason for being can be linked to a particular crisis. Many religious movements within the religions of the great civilizations have had a crisis motivation.

For nonliterate peoples, the most significant crisis producing situation which they have been forced to confront again and again, in the last century at least, is that of modernity borne by colonial and missionary efforts. *Modernity* refers to the conditions and way of life issuing from the industrial, technological, and intellectual revolutions in the Western world during the last century. It has been largely from the perspective of modernity that nonliterate peoples have been incorrectly evaluated as "primitive."

The questions we must face in this chapter center on the importance and effectiveness of such religious activities in helping people meet and survive the confrontation with modernity. We must attempt to appreciate the character of this confrontation from the perspective of nonliterate peoples. We must see how the activities of the crisis cult serve the needs of the people. We should also keep in mind the Indonesian example of Hainuwele, which we discussed in Chapter 5, for it is an example of the transformation and application of origin stories in response to the confrontation with modernity presented by colonists.

THE TANGU SITUATION

The traditional way of life of the Tangu is very differently based than that introduced by European missionaries and colonists. It is in the gap between the two that the crisis occurs, and it is the purpose of the crisis cult to bridge this gap. Let us look closer. The pre-European Tangu were hunters, gardeners, and gatherers. They built thatch-roofed houses of wood on stilts in clearings in the bush. Each year in new gardens each household cultivated yams, bananas, sugarcane, and tobacco. They hunted pigs, cassowaries, and lizards, and they gathered a variety of edible wild leaves, fruits, and nuts. Each family unit and village were self-sufficient. Within the village the distributive system tended toward equality of food and other possessions among all families. At the end of the harvest, for example, a feast was held which, among other things, consumed the portions of the harvest that some families had more of than the others. The peacefulness and friendship among the people of a village were bound to this notion of equivalence; and equivalence extended beyond goods to include morality. Indeed, moral transgressions were expressed in terms of inequivalence, often related to food.

The measure of human worth for the Tangu was tied to the capacity for food production, but even more important was the ability to obtain and maintain equality, and therefore, friendly relations. The measure of human worth was subsequently qualitative rather than quantitative.

Of course, there is every likelihood that situations of crisis which precipitated cultic responses existed among the Tangu long before European influences were known. Burridge and others have warned against regarding the activities of Europeans as the sole cause of cultic movements. But certainly the European presence gave rise to a crisis. Let us review the European activities and how they introduced elements of modernity.

The colonial administration was established to facilitate peaceful colonization of these lands. The administrators' relationship with the Tangu was found in several areas of life. In the economic sphere, they introduced wage labor and cash crops. They had to supervise, select, and train people for specific activities. In the area of health, they established hygienic regulations and medical facilities. To communicate with the people they introduced pidgin English, which became the *lingua franca* of the area, and they taught the Tangu certain methods of keeping written records. Still, the administrators did not live among the Tangu nor spend much time in their villages.

Churches established missions close to the villages and missionaries spent much time with the people. The missionaries directed services of worship, but they also offered education to the Tangu children who were allowed to attend mission schools. Their primary concerns were, of course, to teach Christianity, to convert these people, and to introduce them to modern ways of life. The purpose of education was to permit them to read scripture. Because of their closeness to the native people, missionaries often found themselves in the difficult and awkward position of standing between the Tangu and the administrators. Action on behalf of the interest of either party would alienate the other.

According to Burridge, it is in the framework of this triangle of complex political, economic, and religious affairs that a crisis emerged with the potential of precipitating a cultic movement. The constituents of the crisis can be described in terms of various sets of oppositions which demonstrate the magnitude of the tension.[2]

1. In the most general sense we can see that the European presence introduced an unknown base of power into the Tangu environment. The activities and ways of both the colonial administration and the missionaries were unknown to the Tangu, and they had no basis in their own view of the world for understanding them. Power linked to the possession of material goods and money was alien to the Tangu world view.

2. Through the introduction of wage labor and cash crops, the very underpinnings of Tangu culture were knocked away. This development forced them to confront a measure of human worth on a numerical and quantitative basis. Time was

---

[2] Kenelm Burridge, *New Heaven New Earth: A Study of Millenarian Activities* (New York: Schocken Books, 1969), pp. 143–45.

measured in monetary terms, as was food. Thus, the measure of the worth of a person became money. Money is impersonal, in itself valueless and exchangeable, and unlike food, it can be stored up and passed from generation to generation. The Tangu had to confront a system in which human worth is identified with wealth, wealth measured in terms of quantities of money.

3. These changes were only a part of the introduction of a complex economy where a subsistence economy had existed. Money as the medium of exchange is abstract and transforms the whole character of economics. Economic activities are no longer as personal, nor are they based on a principle of reciprocity. Specialization is increased in labor as well as in economic activities.

4. Where political power had been diffused throughout the community, the Europeans introduced the notion that political power is based on superiority-inferiority distinctions.

5. Although many Tangu readily accepted a great deal of the European ways, they did not initially realize that their participation would never permit them to gain equivalence, and hence, from their point of view, a relationship of friendliness and peacefulness with Europeans.

This list of oppositions could easily be extended. But from this much it is clear that such seemingly minor things as the introduction of money into a culture which previously had a subsistence-type nonmonied economy has repercussions at every level of the culture, even at the very core of its metaphysical assumptions. It completely revises the very basis for determining human worth. With this observation we can begin to appreciate the extent of the crisis felt by the Tangu as a result of the European introduction of modernity.

It must be understood that the crisis did not precipitate cultic activities simply because of the presence of these oppositions. The Tangu engaged a whole range of responses by which to realign their world view and hence regain a state of equality and the peace and friendship which they expected would accompany it. The crisis became critical as the Tangu began to see that they would never be permitted to obtain equivalence with the Europeans.

Against this better understanding of the context of the crisis, we can look again at the rites described at the beginning of this chapter. Burridge provides further helpful insights here. In both rites we can observe adaptations and transformation of traditional actions in order to achieve a new status, a new perspective, and a new way of life, thereby attempting to resolve the crisis.

Burridge tells us that the circle dance rite does not resemble Tangu ritual dance, especially since it is focused upon an individual. Before this the Tangu had never singled out individuals in such situations as dance. In this crisis rite, after establishing unity of cause in the communal feast, individuals seek revelations, and hence a new basis for reality, by entering a state of ecstasy. They attempt symbolically to bring death to their old selves, torn by the state of crisis, by falling on the ground into a trance without apparent life and then by being reborn into a new status informed by their revelation.

Insight into the other rite is also given by Burridge, who found that *coitus interruptus* had been important to Tangu fertility rites. Mixed sexual fluids had been considered essential to the fertility of a garden belonging to the newly married. Thus, the Tangu applied this old means of assuring new life to the crisis situation, since an act to obtain the new life was so desperately needed. It is fitting that the cemetery is chosen in place of the garden, for here rest the ancestors so closely identified with a way of life no longer livable. These practices provide a bridge also to certain European practices observed by the Tangu. The Catholic priests, for example, sprinkled holy water as an agent of purification, blessing, fertilization, and healing. The cultic acts attempted to bring old and new ways together as a new basis for life.[3]

Both of these rites were performed in response to dream revelations and both promised the reward of certain material goods. It is these goods, which are called *cargo,* which symbolize for the Tangu the new situation they desire. They already had limited access to most of these goods, so it was not simply their limited possession that they were ultimately concerned with in these movements. Rather it was that *cargo* had come to symbolize for them the way of life (modernity) which had been introduced to them but in which they were not permitted to fully participate. They did not have access to the source of these goods nor to the way of life represented by the arrival of ships that unloaded their cargoes for the Europeans.

The crisis cults which have taken place in the area of Oceania and Melanesia have been called *cargo cults,* since the people identify their hopes and expectations with the cargoes of the ships from the Western world.

The degree to which literacy became symbolic in the situation is notable. In the precolonial way of life, the peoples of this whole area depended heavily upon the stories of origin for the revelation of the patterns of culture—the methods of horticulture, hunting, house building and so forth—and upon the spiritual communication with ancestors and deities to maintain a fertile and creative life in the physical world. Spiritual communication was essential to life and was enacted through the media of dreams and visions and the occasional use of ritual acts.

Then came the Europeans, who used writing as a basic form of communication. Missionaries dwelt heavily upon the written word as the means of the revelation of God, and the colonial administration used writing to maintain contact with its home country, the source of its supplies. When the cargo arrived by ship it was labeled with tags naming the intended receiver. A frequent part of the cargo revelation was the promise that when the prophesied ship would arrive, the cargo would have tags bearing names of the Tangu, not those of Europeans. From very early in the period of European contact the native peoples began to show a ritualized attitude toward literacy. It was accepted as a spiritual mode of communication. The receipt of goods by the Europeans was proof enough that it worked.

---

[3] Burridge, *Mambu,* pp. 217–22.

According to Burridge, the Tangu associated European goods with *pas* (pidgin for "letter"), for in service to Europeans they often carried *pas* from an official to a store to receive in return certain goods for the official. They repeatedly saw that for the sending of a letter one gained the return of goods, which were distributed and consumed. Letters seemed to accompany all transactions. Consequently, they came to identify *pas* with cargo, as the symbol of the new life they sought.[4]

In other contexts, literacy was blamed for the situation in which the people found themselves. They said that the missionaries were keeping back certain important pages of the bible, and that not knowing the information on these pages was what was keeping them from obtaining cargo.[5]

To this point we have discussed the depth of the crisis which may take place when modernity is introduced into nonliterate cultures. We have begun to show that in their religious response the people are attempting to restructure their fragmented and torn world into a new world of unity, wholeness, and meaning. Closer examination of the stages these movements go through will be essential, but we need now to present a few more examples.

THE VAILALA MADNESS

The movement known as the Vailala Madness took place in 1919 and was only one in a sequence of such movements in the Gulf Division of Papua in New Guinea. In this movement the people became engaged in frenzied activities. They were observed to stand jabbering and gesticulating, the trunks of their bodies moving back and forth and their heads swaying from side to side.

Another manifestation was the use of long heavy poles as instruments of divination. They were supported by two men, but they were said to move by themselves. The pole could move about to find persons guilty of offense or to perform other feats of divination.

The movement was initiated by a prophet named Evara who, wearing a soiled coat of white duck as symbol of his authority, prophesied the coming of a steamer which would bring the people cargo. The steamer would also be carrying the spirits of their dead ancestors, who would return to life. He prophesied that the Europeans would be driven away and that the goods would come to their rightful owners, the Papua. Evara at one point even prophesied the arrival of an airplane.

Christian elements played an important part in this movement. Adherents to the cult called themselves "Jesus Christ men," and many had visions in which they communicated with God or Jesus or learned of heaven or other

[4] *Ibid.,* pp. 193–94.

[5] M. Meggitt, "Uses of Literacy in New Guinea and Melanesia," in *Literacy in Traditional Societies,* ed. Jack Goody (London: Cambridge University Press, 1968), pp. 298–310.

biblical figures or places. The premovement Papuan religious practices suffered, for masks and paraphernalia were destroyed and the rituals were banned. In place of these rituals new ones of European inspiration arose. There were daily feasts for the dead which took place at tables set for their relatives. Special houses were built in which men sat to communicate with the dead. Flagpoles were placed for use as instruments for communicating with one's ancestors.

To the fullest extent possible, former Papuan ways were put aside and declared wicked, and European and Christian ways were adopted. High value was placed on European goods and on the importance of the Christian bible. Many of the people, though not literate, began reading the bible; that is, they walked about "reading" aloud from the bible.

Although European goods and ways were highly valued, there was nonetheless a negative value placed on the Europeans. The "madness" permitted many Papua to confront Europeans with hostilities which otherwise they would never have shown. Spreading rapidly, the movement persisted for several years until it was finally put down by the colonial administration.[6]

The elements introduced in this example are the activities of the prophet, the expectation of the return of the dead, and what amounts to a millennium, that is, the end of the world succeeded by the re-creation of a former perfection with the resurrected dead. These millennial elements are often found in crisis movements, and consequently, *millenarian movement* is a term often used to describe them. The prophet is also a common figure in crisis cults.

THE GHOST DANCE MOVEMENT

Our image of the feather-bonneted horse-mounted warrior of the northern plains in central United States seems perhaps timeless, but the history of the rise and fall of the cultures which this figure represents is a short but dramatic one. Before the eighteenth century, numerous tribes lived along the eastern and western fringes of this great expanse of open grassland. In small bands they hunted the buffalo, which roamed the plains in great herds, and practiced some horticulture. In the early eighteenth century these peoples began to feel the pressure of other Native Americans who were being forced to move westward because of European occupation of land in the east. Coincident with their expulsion from their homelands, numbers of horses began to appear in the northern plains areas. These had been introduced by Spanish colonists in Mexico and the American southwest. Their movement onto the plains joined with their acceptance of the horse was the key to a rapid and widespread rise in the strength and stature of these peoples. From the mid-eighteenth to the mid-nineteenth centuries, these cultures were rich, strong, and proud. The worth of human life was

---

[6] Peter Worsley, *The Trumpet Shall Sound* (New York: Schocken Books, 1957; rev. ed., 1968), pp. 75–90.

FIGURE 7.1. A ghost dance gathering (Arapaho). (Courtesy of Smithsonian Institution, National Anthropological Archives.)

tied to hunting and war. Wealth was measured in horses and the extent of one's family, which were ways of demonstrating physical strength, prowess, skills, knowledge, and spiritual powers.

Then the Europeans came to settle the land, to kill the buffalo, to cross the plains with trails and railroads. The plains peoples were formidable opponents at first, and the wars were long and fierce. But the strength of the Europeans, itself a product of modernity, could never be matched by the native peoples. Eventually these peoples, the herds of buffalo on which they lived, and the land through which they traveled were conquered and destroyed. Those native peoples who had died in the fight were able to find fulfillment in something like the fashion designated by their tradition, for it was honorable to die fighting for one's family and land. But some survived, and they were placed on land reserves held by the United States government. Without any possibility of pursuing life as they had known it, they were now at the mercy of the goodwill of the government agent, the trader, and the missionary. The way of life they had known was dead and along with it the way in which life could be meaningful. Nothing short of a complete and total transformation could resolve the tragedy of this situation. What had been done had to be somehow undone.

As early as the 1850s certain prophets began to speak of visions of the end of the world and the rise of a new order. By the 1870s, the frequency of these prophecies was increasing. Most significant was the rise of the Paiute prophet named Wovoka, who through his visions instituted the ghost dance and prophesied that it would lead to a general catastrophe issuing forth the millennium. In the catastrophe the Europeans would be destroyed as well as the things they had introduced. The native peoples would survive, and their prairies and plains

FIGURE 7.2. The ghost dance of 1893 (Arapaho). (Courtesy of Smithsonian Institution, National Anthropological Archives.)

would be restored and filled with the great herds of buffalo and other animals. The prophet called for the performance of the ghost dance, the secession of fighting, and the institution of "right living."

The rites varied slightly from community to community but centered on a trance dance, not unlike that of the Tangu. The dance was around a pole, and when people fell upon the ground in a trance they were left undisturbed until they were able to tell of their revelation, most commonly a communication from the dead. Often the revelation indicated that the dead were on a journey back to this world. They encouraged the living people to continue their activities, for the millennium was imminent. Some communities adopted special ghost dance shirts to symbolize their situation.[7]

Again we see that it was not simply the confrontation of modernity which precipitated the crisis cult, the millennial expectation; it was the realization of the impossibility of entering modernity while at the same time finding it completely impossible to continue in the old way of life. The crisis cult arose to meet the need for a complete renewal of life and culture.

---

[7] James Mooney, *The Ghost Dance Religion and the Sioux Outbreak of 1890*, Part 2 (Washington, D.C.: 14th Annual Report of the Bureau of American Ethnology, 1896).

THE MAJI MAJI MOVEMENT

Many of the countries in Africa which have gained independence from colonial rule in the last decades can trace the history of their independence to crisis cult movements. These often link militant revolt against colonial rule with religious beliefs and actions, even those introduced by Christian missions.[8]

In the early part of this century a movement known as the Maji Maji Revolt was aimed against German colonial rule in southern Tanzania, known then as German East Africa. The movement centered upon a man by the name of Kinjikitile, who was possessed with a divination spirit as well as a spirit sent by the superior deity, Bokero. Speaking in the context of an oppressive colonial cotton-growing scheme, Kinjikitile prophesied that the dead ancestors would return and that Africans would become free men. He took advantage of the situation to deal Europeans much ridicule. His prophecies were linked with a military uprising, and he called people to him to obtain *maji,* which was a sacred water that would make them invulnerable to the bullets of white men's guns. As Kinjikitile prepared his military forces through training and the dispensing of *maji,* he encouraged a temporary submission to colonial oppression pending his order for the revolt to begin.

In 1905, the revolt erupted with the uprooting of cotton plants and militant action against colonists. The leadership of Kinjikitile was soon discovered, and he was arrested and hanged for his actions. But the revolt, gaining strength from the desires for independence as well as from faith in *maji* and Kinjikitile's prophecy, quickly became widespread and bloody. It lasted for nearly two years. The Germans in order to try to bring them under control finally began to destroy all the food plants on which the Africans depended. It is estimated that perhaps 75,000 Africans lost their lives.

The great devastation and suffering this movement cost the Africans resulted in their denunciation of Kinjikitile for a time. But decades later, African independence movements in this area saw that they were in continuity with Kinjikitile's movement, a continuity which finally led to African independence.

THE PROCESS OF CONFRONTATION AND CRISIS

In a review of the cultic actions arising from confrontations with modernity we can see that they invoke responses which unfold in stages over time. When the elements of modernity are introduced, various individuals within the native culture embrace them, whereas others reject them. The whole culture begins to

---

[8] For examples, see Robert I. Rotberg, *Rebellion in Black Africa* (London: Oxford University Press, 1971).

undergo transformations to accommodate the new situation but on the basis of the old principles, the old world view. Gradually, the failure to achieve accommodation brings about growing dissatisfaction, which is reflected in the oral traditions and in the actions of various individuals. As successive failures begin to demonstrate the impossibility of accommodation or resolution, the crisis reaches a climax. Often at this point a revelation from a source external to the situation is received by a prophet or an ordinary person through a dream. The revelation fuses the general dissatisfaction into a coherent movement further united by the performance of cultic rituals. Generally, this moment quickly dissipates, but the whole cycle is often repeated again and again. Cycles of such activities have been observed for decades in some communities.[9]

To appreciate the character of the crisis and the process by which nonliterate peoples formally respond increases our understanding, but we must still consider why the response so commonly occurs in the ritual forms we have described. Most have explained the ritual performances of these movements as evidence of psychological disorientation or flights into fantasy. These sorts of explanations ignore the effectiveness of ritual and consequently are not entirely satisfying to me.

It seems appropriate that we should consider these religious activities as part of the same fabric as oral traditions, ritual, and the role of the symbols of time and space in religious orientations. Indeed, any belief or practice may become clearest at times of crisis.

In this way we can see that when a nonliterate culture is confronted with modernity, its people are not faced with a simple change of certain practices or methods or even values. They are faced with a change in their entire way of life, in their world view, in their perception of reality, in the basis upon which life is understood to be worth living and is directed toward fulfillment. The complexity and extent of such changes can never be accommodated by those actions in which people attempt to extend their own view of the world to adapt to the new elements now confronting them. Certainly this step is what is initially attempted. But when this approach inevitably fails, nothing short of a total and radical change in world view is possible.

In our earlier discussion of the ritual actions of nonliterate peoples, we found that changes of great magnitude are commonly dealt with in ritual. Such changes as the transformation of a youth to an adult and the conclusion of one year and the beginning of another approach the order required in the crisis. We can recognize in the rituals of the crisis movements the pattern of rites of passage. This is precisely the action called for: The death of one way of life followed by the birth of another. We can recognize the phases of separation, liminality, and reaggregation enacted in the rites of the crisis movements. We can easily identify the symbolism of death and rebirth. Symbols of death may

---

[9] For further discussion, see Burridge, *New Heaven New Earth*, pp. 105–16.

take many forms: the destruction of clothing (native or European), the abandonment of fields, the departure from homes, the abandonment of worship and education at the mission, the entrance into a semiconscious state or trance. The phase and conditions of liminality are also clearly present. It can be recognized in nudity, in special clothing like the ghost dance shirt, in the ritual space created by the erection of a pole or the construction of special buildings, in the abandonment of social restrictions and the extraordinary use of sexuality. Prophets virtually personify liminality. They usually are not members of the community they serve, and they receive their authority from outside the ordinary structures of society. The structures into which the liminal are reborn are usually those set forth by a prophet. In the short run the people who accept a prophet have high expectations and anticipate the arrival of "cargo," the millennial catastrophe, or the initiation of the new order. As these expectations fade, they remain active by continuing to shape the memories, the hopes, and the motivations which make life possible.

Crisis cults usually fail, at least in the specific terms in which they are stated. The ship does not arrive; the world does not end; the dead do not arise. But the movements may succeed in the long run, by bringing about the gradual transformation of world view which is necessary for nonliterate peoples to enter modernity and to do so in a way that is finally true to their own heritage.

The success of these cults and their rituals is that they permit the tradition to persist, although in transformed ways. They permit the people to retain their identity, their sense of worth, their hold on reality, and at the same time to undergo the radical changes necessary to meet the severe confrontations modernity presents to their way of life, and finally to accept and affirm certain changes. In short, the survival of the fundamental character and identity of the community is often due to these religious movements.

8

concluding remarks

In the thousands of centuries of human existence, it is in this particular century, it is in our lifetimes, that we see the end of the widespread existence of small-scale nonliterate cultures which sustain themselves by hunting and gathering, fishing, or small-scale agriculture. We can scarcely imagine the scale of the effects which developments in technology and science have brought on peoples in every corner of the globe. Although it was perhaps not the intention of the developments we know as modernity to do so, they have nonetheless produced as a by-product the virtual extinction of small-scale societies of nonliterate peoples with subsistence economies. Doubtless our response to this development is one of mixed emotions. On the one hand we applaud this as an unprecedented achievement, as one of the fruits of progress; yet we may also have nostalgic feelings in which we hold to the somewhat romantic notion that it is a pity that the "natives" have not been left alone to continue in their own ways, untainted by modernity.

Of comparable significance is the fact that the knowledge we have of archaic peoples and contemporary nonliterate peoples has for the most part been gained in the last one hundred years. During this period of time there has been an intense effort to investigate and to record these cultures, and much of the data produced pertain to the study of the religions of nonliterate peoples. This effort has been largely that of various branches of anthropology. But as these cultures undergo broad transformations and enter modernity, ethnographers and anthropologists are entering their own crisis. Their traditional subjects threaten to become their colleagues. Students of religion have generally dispensed with the study of the religions of nonliterate peoples for several reasons. One view would hold that the understanding of a religious tradition must come from a face-to-face interchange with the adherents of the religion, an approach which becomes increasingly difficult as these cultures are transformed by modernity. Another view would hold that these cultures do not really have religions in any sense comparable to the great traditions of world religions. One version of this position would argue that the beliefs and actions of these cultures are not yet developed to the stage of being classified as religious but rather are based upon erroneous beliefs in the compulsive powers of magic.

The most general concern of this book has been to demonstrate: (1) the immense variety of religions which may be found among nonliterate cultures and (2) the complexity and sophistication of the religious beliefs and expressions. We have shown that these religious systems are comparable in many ways to those of literate peoples and to the great religious traditions which have a worldwide influence. And we have found that the religions of nonliterate peoples are not different in kind, nor in any single distinguishing feature, from the rest of the religions of humankind. However, this is not to say that there are not distinctions to be made nor that all religions are the same. Indeed, we have seen that there is a whole set of religious categories in which certain tendencies may often be associated with nonliterate peoples. Furthermore, we have shown that at least one way to address and understand these tendencies is to focus on the fact of nonliteracy, the lack of a written counterpart to the spoken language. Yet we fully acknowledge that this tie is perhaps only one of many ways these tendencies may be meaningfully associated and understood.

Nonliteracy is linked with limits on the potential size of a culture, its forms of economy and political system, its modes of thought, and its forms of expression. Nonliteracy also shapes conceptions of time and space, fundamental to the process of religious conception and expression. We can see this fact clearly when we consider the various forms which are so ingeniously used to express complex ideas—art, artifacts, architecture, colors, odors, verbal arts, and symbolic movements. We can see how belief is both shaped by and expressed through the most commonplace aspects of sustenance activities. Nonliteracy shapes relationships and orientations within time. It encourages the face-to-face, person-to-person transmission of culture in forms especially appropriate to the needs of such processes—stories, songs, prayers, and other aspects of oral tradition.

The constraints as well as the freedoms which are a part of cultures because of nonliteracy must also be dealt with by the student of religions. There are no written documents to analyze and interpret other than written records created by outsiders. One has no choice but to take a cultural approach to the study of these religions, for it is principally in broad cultural forms that we have evidence pertaining to religion.

Consequently, we are faced with great opportunities and challenges in the study of nonliterate peoples. The opportunities rest upon extending our knowledge of the dimensions of religious belief and practice in the cultural domains where religion is lived by all the people of a culture, a dimension to which in nonliterate cultures we are nearly confined. This cultural dimension exists in religions everywhere, but it has been largely ignored by religion scholars because of a preference to study religion in terms of its written documents. We are presented with the challenge to learn how to read and to understand the religious significance of elements of expression that are not written, such things as art, architecture, oral traditions, and ritual.

Bibliography

It must be emphasized that the religions of nonliterate peoples have been documented in published works for a long time. Especially since the nineteenth century, when ethnography began to play a major role as a human science, has there been a deluge of published documents about nonliterate peoples the world over. This book is in no way an attempt to systematically present the religions of all or any of these cultures, but it remains important to provide at least initial bibliographical aids before we turn to the suggestions for general works, which provide further reading on the perspectives and subjects I have presented in this book.

Perhaps the most readily available general bibliography of important ethnographies is Raoul Naroll et al., "A Standard Ethnographic Sample: Preliminary Edition," *Current Anthropology*, Vol. 11, No. 2 (1970), 235–48. Also helpful is the section of "Selected Monographs on Non-Western Religious Systems" in William A. Lessa and Evon Z. Vogt, eds. *Reader in Comparative Religion*, 4th ed., (New York: Harper & Row Publishers, Inc., 1979), pp. 463–71.

For more extensive access to ethnographic data the following bibliographies and sources are helpful. Robert V. Kemper and John F. S. Phinney, *History of Anthropology, A Research Bibliography* (New York: Garland Pub., 1977) and International Committee for Social Science Information and Documentation, *International Bibliography of Social and Cultural Anthropology* (Chicago: Aldine Publishing Company, published annually beginning in 1955). The *Human Relations Area Files* (New Haven, Conn.: Human Relations Area Files, Inc.) is an invaluable source of information. Data indexed for comparison on many aspects and features of culture are maintained for cultures the world over. The principal guide and bibliography for these files are George P. Murdock, et al., *Outline of Cultural Materials*, 4th ed. (New Haven, Conn.: Human Relations Area Files, Inc., 1971) and George P. Murdock, *Outline of World Cultures*, 5th ed. (New Haven, Conn.: Human Relations Area Files, Inc., 1975).

Recent texts on the religions of nonliterate peoples within major geographic areas written from the perspective of the study of religion are Benjamin C. Ray, *African Religions: Symbol, Ritual, and Community* (Englewood Cliffs, N.J.: Prentice-Hall, Inc., 1976); and Sam D. Gill, *Native American Religions: An Introduction* (Belmont, Cal.: Wadsworth Publishing Co., Inc., 1982). These provide bibliographical aids and suggested readings.

The following readings for each chapter in the book generally do not duplicate those suggested in the notes to each chapter. Consult chapter notes for suggested readings for the specific subjects dealt with. The following suggestions are intended to provide readings relative to the general background of each chapter.

CHAPTER 1

EVANS-PRITCHARD, E. E. *Theories of Primitive Religion.* London: Oxford University Press, 1965. A valuable critical presentation of the classical theories by which the religions of nonliterate peoples have been understood.

GOODY, JACK. *The Domestication of the Savage Mind.* London: Cambridge University Press, 1977. An excellent discussion of nonliteracy as a mode of communication and the effects modes of communication have upon culture.

———*Literacy in Traditional Societies.* London: Cambridge University Press, 1968. A collection of essays related to the acquisition of literacy. Especially valuable is the essay by Goody and Watt.

MONTAGU, ASHLEY. *The Concept of the Primitive.* New York: The Free Press, 1968. A collection of important articles.

CHAPTER 2

DOUGLAS, MARY. *Purity and Danger: An Analysis of Concepts of Pollution and Taboo.* Baltimore, Md.: Penguin Books, 1966. A study of the significance and consequences of being out of place.

ELIADE, MIRCEA. *The Sacred and the Profane: The Nature of Religion.* New York: Harper & Row, Publishers, Inc., 1959. An introduction to the notions of the religious significance of the categories of time and space.

——— *Images and Symbols: Studies in Religious Symbolism.* New York: Sheed & Ward, Inc., 1961. An analysis of religious symbols of time and space.

LEACH, EDMUND. "Two Essays Concerning the Symbolic Representation of Time." in *Rethinking Anthropology,* pp. 124–36. London: Athlone Press, University of London, 1961. Introductory articles on the nature of time.

LEVI-STRAUSS, CLAUDE. *The Savage Mind..* Chicago: The University of Chicago Press, 1966. This book investigates the minds of nonliterate peoples.

SCOTT, NATHAN. "Mimesis and Time in Modern Literature," in *The Broken Center,* pp. 25–76. New Haven, Conn.: Yale University Press, 1966. An excellent introduction to Western views of time.

SMITH, JONATHAN Z. "The Influence of Symbols on Social Change: A Place on Which to Stand." In *Map Is Not Territory,* pp. 129–46. Leiden, The Netherlands: E. J. Brill, 1978. A discussion of the notion of place in religious symbolism.

——— "The Wobbling Pivot." in *Map Is Not Territory,* pp. 88–103. Leiden, The Netherlands: E. J. Brill, 1978. A critical evaluation, with suggestions for development, of Eliade's notions of sacred time and space.

TUAN, YI-FU. *Space and Place: The Perspective of Experience.* Minneapolis: University of Minnesota Press, 1977. A good general introduction to the notion of place.

CHAPTER 3

CARPENTER, EDMUND. *Eskimo Reality.* New York: Holt, Rinehart & Winston, 1973. This book integrates the analysis of world view and art.

DOCKSTADER, FREDERICK J. *Indian Art in America.* Greenwich, Conn.: New York Graphic Society, 1961; and *Indian Art of the Americas.* New York: Museum of the American Indian, Heye Foundation, 1973. These books provide a basic survey of Native American art forms and history.

HOLM, BILL, AND BILL REID. *Indian Art of the Northwest Coast: A Dialogue on Craftsmanship and Aesthetics.* Seattle: University of Washington Press, 1975. Art produced by the peoples native to the American Pacific northwest coast is described and discussed by craftsmen, thus providing a rare perspective. The book has an important introduction by Edmund Carpenter.

JOPLING, CAROL F., ed. *Aesthetics in Primitive Societies: A Critical Anthology.* New York: E. P. Dutton, 1971. An anthology of essays by noted scholars on the art and aesthetics of nonliterate peoples with examples drawn from most of the major culture areas.

THOMPSON, ROBERT F. *African Art in Motion.* Berkeley and Los Angeles: University of California Press, 1974. This is a major advance in the consideration of the significance and meaning of the arts of nonliterate peoples. It views them in their context of cultural values, which centers on motion.

WILLETT, FRANK. *African Art: An Introduction.* New York: Praeger Publishers, Inc., 1971. A good introduction to African art, with illustrations and an extensive bibliography.

CHAPTER 4

ELIADE, MIRCEA. *A History of Religious Ideas.* Volume 1: *From the Stone Age to the Eleusinian Mysteries.* Chicago: University of Chicago Press, 1979. Includes a good general survey of the archaic period in the history of religions.

JAMES, E. O. *Prehistoric Religion.* London: Thames and Hudson, 1957. An overview of the data from this period.

MARINGER, JOHANNES. *The Gods of Prehistoric Man.* New York: Alfred A. Knopf, 1960. An analysis of the religions of the stone age.

CHAPTER 5

DORSON, RICHARD M., ed. *African Folklore.* Garden City, N.Y.: Anchor Books, 1972. Dorson's article is of great value, as are the other essays in this collection.

"ORAL CULTURES AND ORAL PERFORMANCES." *New Literary History,* Volume VIII, No. 3 (1977). This special issue contains essays by noted scholars on oral traditions.

PELTON, ROBERT. *The Trickster in West Africa: A Study of Mythic Ironies and Sacred Delight.* Berkeley: University of California Press, 1980. An excellent new study of the trickster figure.

CHAPTER 6

ELIADE, MIRCEA. *Rites and Symbols of Initiation.* New York: Harper & Row, Publishers, Inc., 1958. A study of various aspects of initiation ritual based on many diverse accounts.

────── *Shamanism: Archaic Techniques of Ecstasy.* Princeton, N.J.: Princeton University Press, 1964. The most comprehensive and authoritative work on the subject.

MUNN, NANCY. "Symbolism in a Ritual Context: Aspects of Symbolic Action." In John J. Honigmann, *Handbook of Social and Cultural Anthropology.* Chicago: Rand McNally

& Company, 1973. A valuable essay on social scientists' views of the study of ritual and ritual symbolism.

MYERHOFF, BARBARA G., AND SALLY F. MOORE, eds. *Secular Ritual.* Assen, The Netherlands: Van Gorcum, 1977. A collection of essays considering ritual as both religious and secular, which therefore helps to establish that important distinction.

SHAUGHNESSY, JAMES D., ed. *The Roots of Ritual.* Grand Rapids, Mich.: William B. Eerdmans Publishing Company, 1973. A valuable collection of essays about various aspects of ritual by noted scholars.

TURNER, VICTOR. *The Forest of Symbols: Aspects of Ndembu Ritual.* Ithaca, N.Y.: Cornell University Press, 1967. An important collection of essays by one of the outstanding students of ritual symbolism.

——— *The Ritual Process: Structure and Anti-Structure.* Chicago: Aldine Publishing Co., 1969. A seminal study of the structure of ritual processes.

VAN GENNEP, ARNOLD. *The Rites of Passage.* London: Routledge and Kegan Paul, 1960. A classic study of rites of passage.

CHAPTER 7

BURRIDGE, KENELM. *New Heaven New Earth: A Study of Millenarian Activities.* New York: Schocken Books, 1967. A study of the causes and structure of millenarian activities, including a survey of the primary interpretive perspectives which have been used by scholars.

LaBARRE, WESTON. "Materials for a History of Studies of Crisis Cults: A Bibliographic Essay." *Current Anthropology.* Vol. 12, No. 1 (1971), 3-44. A comprehensive bibliography of studies of crisis cults.

TURNER, HAROLD W. *Bibliography of New Religious Movements in Primal Societies.* Boston: G. K. Hall & Co., 1978. Volume I is on Africa; Volume II is on North America. An extensive bibliography.

WILSON, BRYAN R. *Magic and the Millennium: A Sociological Study of Religious Movements of Protest Among Tribal and Third-World Peoples.* New York: Harper & Row, Publishers, Inc., 1973. This insightful and comprehensive study interprets these movements in the context of sociological theory.

WORSLEY, PETER. *The Trumpet Shall Sound: A Study of "Cargo" Cults in Melanesia.* London: Macgibbon and Kee, 1957. A classic work on cargo cults.

Index